Connecting a Continent

The Story of America's Canals

**Ray Spangenburg
and Diane K. Moser**

REPLICA BOOKS
A DIVISION OF BAKER & TAYLOR
BRIDGEWATER, NJ

FIRST REPLICA BOOKS EDITION, AUGUST 1999

Published by Replica Books, a division of Baker & Taylor,
1200 Route 22 East, Bridgewater, NJ 08807

Replica Books is a trademark of Baker & Taylor

Biographical Note

This Replica books edition, first published in 1999, is an
unabridged republication of the work first published by
Facts on File, New York in 1992

Baker & Taylor Cataloging-in-Publication Data

Spangenburg, Ray, 1939-
The story of America's canals / Ray Spangenburg
and Diane K. Moser. —1st Replica Books ed.
p.   cm.
ISBN 073510204X
Originally published: New York : Facts on File, c1992.
(Connecting a continent)
Includes bibliographical references and index.
SUMMARY: Traces the history of canals and canal building
in America, from the first American canals to the building
of the Panama Canal and the recent work done on the Illinois
Waterway.
1. Canals - United States - History - Juvenile literature.
2. Canals - United States - Design and construction -
Juvenile literature. 3. Panama Canal (Panama) - History -
Juvenile literature. [1. Canals - History. 2. Panama Canal
(Panama) - History.] I. Moser, Diane, 1944-   II. Title.
TC623.S63 1999
386'.4/0973—dc 21

Manufactured in the United States of America

· CONNECTING · A · CONTINENT ·

THE STORY OF
AMERICA'S
CANALS

**Ray Spangenburg
and Diane K. Moser**

Facts On File
New York • Oxford

The Story of America's Canals
Copyright © 1992 by Ray Spangenburg and Diane K. Moser

Facts On File, Inc.
460 Park Avenue South
New York, NY 10016
USA

Facts On File Limited
c/o Roundhouse Publishing Ltd.
P.O. Box 140
Oxford OX2 7SF
United Kingdom

Text and jacket design by Donna Sinisgalli
Composition by Facts On File, Inc.

Printed in the United States of America

10 9 8 7 6 5 4 3 2 1

This book is printed on acid-free paper.

In memory of Casey,
always happily underfoot at computer and bookcase,
a loyal companion
and the best dog we ever had

CONTENTS

Acknowledgments   ix

1.   Creating Waterways: A Brief History of Canal Building   1

2.   The First American Canals, 1790–1803   5

3.   Building the Erie Canal, 1777–1825   15

4.   The Boom Days, 1825–1850   27

5.   Construction Continues: A Losing Race with the Iron Horse, 1825–1840   35

6.   Canals Come to the Midwest—All But Too Late: Indiana and Illinois   45

7.   From Sea to Sea: The Panama Canal, 1870–1914   53

8.   Canals Continue: Inland Waterways in the 20th Century   65

Glossary   75
Bibliography   77
Index   79

Acknowledgments

We'd like to thank the many individuals, too numerous to name, who helped us on this project—we greatly appreciated both their aid and enthusiasm. In particular, a big thank you to William Shank of the American Canal Society for allowing us to tap his wealth of information and photographs. A special thanks also to Liz Nolley for her ever-cheerful attention to detail and to James Warren, our editor at Facts On File, for his many insightful suggestions in shaping this series.

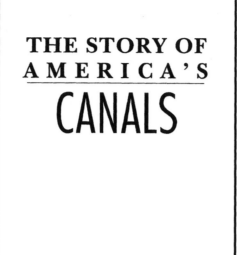

THE STORY OF
AMERICA'S
CANALS

1

CREATING WATERWAYS:
A BRIEF HISTORY OF EARLY CANAL BUILDING

I t's often said that prehistoric humans took their first giant step forward when they learned to use fire. Another great leap occurred when people first learned to conquer water, when some unrecorded early human probably made the first bridge by extending a fallen log over a small creek. And we can only

The 150-mile "Canal du Midi," or Languedoc Canal, built in southern France in 1681 to connect the Mediterranean Sea with the Atlantic Ocean. This illustration, which shows a boat traveling upstream via a lock, was originally published in Denis Diderot's Pictorial Encyclopedia *in 1762.* Bob Mayo and the American Canal and Transportation Center

How a Lock Works

Building a canal can be relatively easy if a water source is close at hand; if the ground is easily channeled, yet firm; and if the land is level. Constructing a canal through hilly country, though, is another story. In fact, hills, inclines and mountain ranges present the greatest engineering challenge of all—usually overcome by a lock (watertight compartment) or series of locks, big enough to hold a boat. Except when they used an innovative system known as an inclined plane (see Chapter 2), most canal builders constructed locks, like stair steps, to move boats uphill or downhill past steep inclines, rapids or falls.

The first known pound-lock, or conventional lock with gates at each end, dates back to China in 984 A.D. and locks were used in the Netherlands at least as far back as the 14th century. Basically, a series of locks function as steps up or down a hillside. Each lock is a compartment with watertight gates at each end. The basic principle at work is simple: Water seeks its own level. A boat enters at the lower level through an open gate, which is closed behind the boat. The fill valve opens, allowing water to flow into the lock until the boat is raised to the upper level. Then the upper gate is opened and the boat passes, or "locks through."

To go down a steep incline, water is pumped into the lock until it is equal with the higher level. The lower gate remains closed while the upper gate opens and the boat enters the lock from upstream, with the upper gate closing behind. The drain valve is opened, the water level lowers, and the lower gate is opened so that the boat can continue on down the canal.

The process could take place very rapidly. British naval captain Frederick Marryat, who traveled the Erie and Oswego canals in 1837, gave this description of "locking through" during the heyday of canal transportation in America:

> The locks did not detain us long—they never lose time in America. When the boat had entered the lock, and the gate was closed upon her, the water was let off with a rapidity which considerably affected her level, and her bows pointed downwards. I timed one lock with a fall of fifteen feet. From the time the gate was closed behind us until the lower one was opened for our egress, was exactly one minute and a quarter; and the boat sank down in the lock so rapidly as to give you the idea that she was scuttled and sinking. . . .

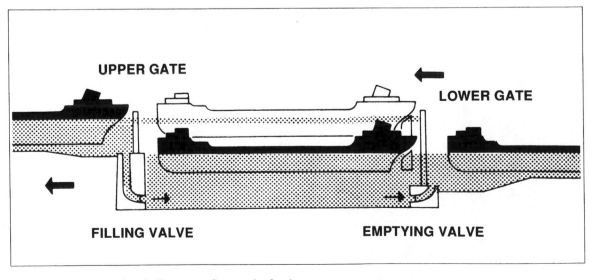

A modern lock in operation. St. Lawrence Seaway Authority

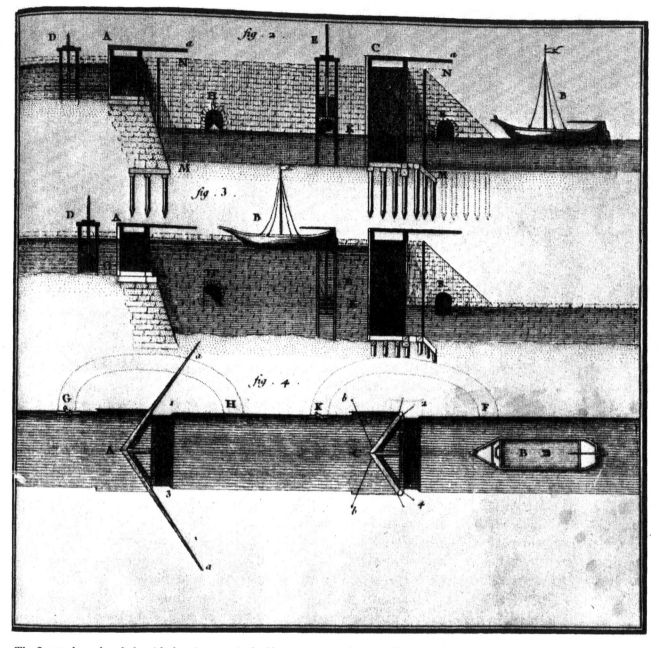

The first truly modern lock, with the miter gate (a double gate swinging horizontally), as designed by Leonardo da Vinci in Milan about 1485. Bob Mayo and the American Canal and Transportation Center

imagine—and admire—that other unknown person long ago who, probably using a sharp stone or stick, first dug a narrow channel in the dirt to direct the flow of water from one place to another. This simple ditch was the ancient ancestor of the canal.

A canal is a waterway made by people—and at its simplest it can be thought of as an artificial stream, creek or river cut into the earth. Canals can be created in many ways, simple to complex, and have many uses. They can be made to carry water to locations where none existed before, perhaps to irrigate farmlands or create artificial lakes. Or they can be built to drain water, drying out marshlands or swamps, or carrying polluted water away. They can also be used to carry people or materials from one place to another. These canals, generally called "transportation canals," are the subject of this book. We'll explore how these waterways, created by people, helped provide transportation for goods, materials and people in America—how they were built, how they connected areas and how they contributed to the growth of the nation.

THE EARLIEST CANALS

The historic record of canal building stretches far back to the days of ancient Mesopotamia. One of the oldest known maps, drawn on a fragile clay tablet, shows two of the world's earliest canals cutting through the ancient city of Nippur on the Euphrates River.

In Persia, some time around 510 B.C., King Darius I ordered a canal built that would link the Nile River with the Red Sea. Stretching nearly 40 miles, this ancient forerunner of today's Suez Canal was 40 feet deep and nearly 100 feet wide. Around the same time canal builders constructed many other short canals throughout the Middle East—mostly for irrigation and drainage, but possibly also for navigation.

The early Chinese, too, were canal builders. Records show that they constructed canals as early as the sixth and fifth centuries B.C. In or around 215 B.C. a 90-mile-long canal was built from the Han capital of Ch'ang-an to the Yellow River. And in about 70 A.D. the Chinese began the first cuts of an enormous canal project that continued through later dynasties and eventually became the Great Canal system, stretching nearly 1,000 miles and linking together most of the major Chinese rivers and populated inland regions.

The Greeks and Romans also built numerous canals throughout northern Europe and Britain, which they used mainly for military transportation. When the Roman Empire fell, European interest in canal building also receded. But by the 12th century A.D. people had begun building canals again.

In fact, some historians estimate that nearly 85% of the transportation in the medieval world was by canal.

Even today the picturesque canals that form the major mode of transportation in Venice, Italy bear the marks of their original medieval construction.

Although the Chinese probably used a primitive form of canal lock or system for raising and lowering boats over hills and inclines, improvements in locks made by the Dutch sometime in the middle to late 1300s allowed canals to be constructed not just across plains and valleys but also through more elevated and varied terrain.

During the 17th century important canals, including the Orléans and Lanquedoc canals, were constructed in France. And in the 18th century a vast system of canals was built in Russia to connect the city of St. Petersburg with the Caspian Sea.

England's great era of canal building began with the Industrial Revolution in the late 18th century. A few small canals had been constructed previously, the first during the reign of King Henry I, tying together the Trent and Witham rivers in 1134. But by the late 1700s the urgent need to transport coal from mines to the growing factories and ports led to England's great boom in canal construction.

During the later years of the 18th century and the early years of the 19th, a vast system of canals was dug throughout the English countryside. The Industrial Revolution—when mechanization began to change the way products were manufactured and transported—dramatically and forever changed England and the world. The combination of coal and canals fed that change and made it possible.

No wonder, then, that across the ocean Americans began looking at their own towns, cities and waterways and dreamed of building connections that would bring wealth and prosperity to their vast and promising new continent.

2

THE FIRST AMERICAN CANALS
1790–1803

Between 1790 and 1840 more than 4,400 miles of canals were built in America. If all that canal mileage had gone into one long canal, it would stretch from the Hudson River in New York City to the San Francisco Bay in California. It wasn't all one long canal though, and, in fact, most of the canals built in the United States before the Erie Canal (1817–1825) were very short.

Early America was a nation greatly in need of transportation. Just beyond the horizon there were always new opportunities, new dreams, new lands to be conquered. Although roads were being built and improved, they remained, for the most part, rough and primitive. Early wagon traffic was slow and costly. What the nation had, though, was waterways, a great ocean, rivers, bays and lakes. What it had, too, was an abundance of visionaries. Looking at the waterways, these visionaries imagined invisible connections.

"What if those two rivers could be connected? Then you could go from X to Y without having to portage, carrying boats and cargo over land."

"What if that lake could be connected to that river? That river to that bay? That lake to that lake?"

Typical of these visionaries was the French explorer Louis Joliet, the co-discoverer of the Mississippi River, who as far back as 1674 had envisioned a short canal across the land bridge between the Illinois River and Lake Michigan. As Father Pierre Dabon, a Jesuit who was the official chronicler on Joliet's expedition in search of the Mississippi, wrote in 1674:

> According to the researches and explorations of Joliet, we can easily to go Florida in boats and by a very good navigation with slight improvement. There will be but one canal to make—and that by cutting only one-half league of prairie from the lake of the Illinois [Lake Michigan] into the St. Louis [now called the Illinois] River, which empties into the Mississippi.

As Joliet foresaw, such a canal—which didn't actually get built for nearly 200 years—could open up a waterway extending from the lake, down the Illinois and into the mighty Mississippi to the Gulf of Mexico.

Typical, too, was a young surveyor named George Washington who envisioned an entire system of canals throughout Virginia that would connect Richmond on Chesapeake Bay with the Ohio River, some 300 miles away. The plan included creating a navigable waterway between the James River in Virginia and the Kanawha River in what is now West Virginia.

In fact, George Washington was instrumental in organizing the James River Canal Company, of which he became honorary president in 1785. The company's first objective was to build short canals and locks around the falls and rapids of the James River, making the river more easily navigable as the initial step in Washington's grand plan. The first of these, a

Loads of bark from New Hampshire being offloaded to ox carts at a landing on the Middlesex Canal in Massachusetts. Middlesex Canal Association

seven-mile canal connecting the city of Richmond with the head of the falls at Westham, was completed in 1790. It was large enough to permit small boats to make their way around the falls and proceed upriver as far as Lynchburg, and by 1795 it was expanded to accommodate bigger freight boats, which brought great loads of wheat, barley, flax, smoked hams, tobacco, whiskey and pork out to market from the Great Valley of Virginia.

For the isolated small communities and farmers in the inland regions of the growing nation the idea of a network of canals linking them with markets and suppliers had become highly attractive. By 1790 nearly 30 different canal companies had incorporated in eight of the original 13 states.

EARLY CANALS IN THE SOUTH

Many of the canals built between 1790 and 1817, like the canals on the James River, were simple navigational improvements circumnavigating falls or rapids along existing waterways. Among the most impressive of these works, however, was a project constructed by the Patowmack Company in Virginia (on whose board

George Washington also served). The undertaking began as a series of small canals around trouble spots on the Potomac River, making it easier to move boats both up and down the river. Starting in 1786, over 200 slave laborers forged canals around Great Falls a few miles above Georgetown and at Little Falls. By the time it was finished in 1802, the improvements to travel on the Potomac included five separate canals. The longest was at Little Falls, running 3,814 feet; the most technically sophisticated were the five locks built at Great Falls.

Beginning in 1787, the Great Dismal Swamp Land Company, also known somewhat colorfully as the "Adventurers for Draining the Great Dismal Swamp," started its own ambitious project through a bleak area stretching across the Virginia and North Carolina border between Norfolk and Elizabeth City on Albemarle Sound (across from Kitty Hawk). The promoters planned a canal that would not only cut through the swamp, opening up an inland water route between North Carolina farmers and busy Virginia ports, but would also allow drainage and reclamation of vast portions of the heavily wooded swamp.

The initial plan called for a shallow canal to be constructed northward from the Pasquotank River to Deep Creek, six miles west of Norfolk on the Chesapeake Bay.

Always a canal enthusiast, George Washington visited the site and pledged $500 to help get things going. Like its other Southern predecessors, the Dismal Swamp Canal had an on-again, off-again construction history. Financed with private funds, the canal always had money problems, and the work, done by slaves in the mosquito- and snake-infested swamp, was slow, tedious and treacherous. Once finished in 1828, though, the canal was a complete success and became, as its promoters had hoped, a major transportation route between northeastern North Carolina and the big Virginia ports. A major side benefit of the project was the discovery that shingles hacked out of the felled juniper trees in the swamp proved much longer lasting that those made of other woods. Bands of wildcatting "shingle-getters" poured into the swamp, and soon profitable boatloads of shingles joined the other cargo heading up the canal to Virginia ports.

Today boats still glide up and down the Dismal Swamp Canal—which has now become part of the Intracoastal Waterway, a continuous series of interconnected rivers, canals and protected bays that boats can use to travel the Atlantic and Gulf coasts without braving the dangerous ocean and gulf waters. Travelers can still see the old towpath, now overgrown by vines and weeds, where in the early days—before boats had motors—horses, mules and oxen walked along the bank, towing the boats through the canal waters.

Five years after construction began on the swamp canal, another major Southern canal project was in the works. Built to connect the Cooper and Santee rivers in South Carolina, the Santee-Cooper Canal, or the "Santee," as it was popularly known, was 22 miles long. Intended to bring increased cargo traffic into Charleston Harbor, the Santee Canal was the most expensive built at the time, eventually costing more than $1 million with a labor force of over 1,000 slaves.

The James River and Kanawha Canal at Balcony Falls in the Blue Ridge Mountains. First envisioned in 1785 by George Washington, this section of the canal was not begun until 1824. Virginia State Library

Early American Canals

1623–1803

1623   Miles Standish suggests cutting a canal across the Isthmus of Cape Code in Massachusetts.

1674   French explorer Louis Joliet envisions a canal from the Illinois River to Lake Michigan.

1783–95   Little Falls Canal
A one-mile canal with five locks built around the rapids on the Mohawk River at Little Falls, New York.

1786–1802 The Patowmack Canal
Built by the Patowmack Company at Great Falls above Georgetown, Virginia.

1787–1828 Dismal Swamp Canal
Originally surveyed by George Washington and Fielding Lewis in 1763 to provide passage from North Carolina to markets and seaports in Virginia.

1790   James River Canal
Promoted by George Washington and John Marshall, authorized by the Virginia Legislature in 1772 to circumvent the falls of the James and Potomac rivers. The first canal, seven miles long and wide enough only for small boats, connected the basin of the James at Richmond to the head of the falls at Westham, Virginia.

1792–94   Schuylkill and Susquehanna Canal
The first 15 miles to connect the Schuylkill and Susquehanna rivers in Pennsylvania are completed in two years, exhausting funds—with no more work done for 27 years. Later known as the Union Canal.

1792–97   Conewago Canal
A one-mile bypass around York Haven Falls on the lower Susquehanna in Pennsylvania—its locks allow two-way traffic for the first time.

1792–1800 Santee Canal
In South Carolina, connecting the Santee and Cooper rivers.

1793–94   South Hadley Falls Canal
On the Connecticut River, two miles long.

1794   Carondelet Canal
Built to connect Spanish-held New Orleans with the Gulf of Mexico. Acquired by the United States with the Louisiana Purchase in 1803.

1794–1803 Middlesex Canal
Built to join Boston Harbor with the Merrimack River at Lowell, Massachusetts, 27½ miles long.

The Santee was beset with problems throughout its construction history. Some were political, such as the stiff opposition mounted by farmers who grew rice along the right-of-way—they feared that the canal would drain their fields. Others came from builder John Christian Senf's single-minded determination to do things his own way. A highly thought of engineer from Sweden, Senf had originally come to America with Hessian troops (who fought on the British side) during the Revolutionary War and had been captured by the Americans at the surrender at Saratoga. He tended toward strong and unbending opinions, and one of his most controversial decisions was to build the canal following a high, dry ridge instead of along one of the Santee's tributaries. As a result, much of the canal was shallow and unnavigable during the summer months until several artificial reservoirs were added later, providing a water supply during the dry season.

Finished in 1800, the Santee Canal brought indigo, rice and, later, cotton out of the interior, safely bypassing the swampy lower Santee River and the treacherous sea voyage from the mouth of the Santee to Charleston Harbor. It was the nation's first true cross-country canal and, despite its high cost, it finally paid off, making a key connection for the farmers and shippers of South Carolina.

The very short Carondelet Canal, less than two miles long and only 15 feet wide, at New Orleans, Louisiana, made a profit almost immediately. Constructed in 1794, the Carondelet helped to make New Orleans (at that time controlled by the Spanish) a major trading port by connecting it directly to the Gulf of Mexico via Bayou St. John and Lake Pontchartrain. Once in operation, the Carondelet quickly saw a steady stream of small-boat traffic carrying cattle, fish and lumber in from the gulf while an equally steady stream of plantation products flowed outward.

EARLY YANKEE CANALS

Not all of the early American canals were built in the South. In the North the "ingenious Yankees," too, had long seen the possibilities of canals. As early as 1623, Miles Standish proposed cutting a canal through the Isthmus of Cape Cod, and in 1724 a New York surveyor named Cadwallader Colden even suggested that a canal might be dug between the Hudson River at Albany and Lake Erie at Buffalo, New York.

New England's oldest canal was built at South Hadley Falls on the Connecticut River in Massachusetts. Begun in 1793 and finished a year later, the two-mile-long canal included the first inclined plane in America. Loammi Baldwin, a prominent New England leader and canal proponent, described the intriguing contraption in his correspondence:

The little South Hadley ditch was noteworthy also because it built the first inclined plane in America—two hundred and thirty feet long with a vertical lift of

The seal of the Proprietors of Locks and Canals showing the inclined plane at Hadley Falls. William Shank

fifty-three feet. The face of the plane was stone, covered with heavy plank. The body of the car (which was raised and lowered at will) was a water-tight box with folding gates at each end. Two water wheels sixteen feet in diameter on either side of the channel at the head of the plane were operated by water from the canal, and pulled the car up or let it down, according as the gears were shifted. Boats floated directly into the car; the gates were then closed behind it and the car emptied water through sluices at the sides. The carriage was then pulled up or let down the plane on three sets of wheels, like the big wagon wheels, graduated in size so as to hold the car exactly level.

The Hadley Falls Canal was an immediate success. It was the first of a series of short canals built to improve navigation along the heavily traveled Connecticut River. Carved out of solid rock, it was an engineering marvel—300 feet long, with towering vertical walls 40 feet deep.

The South Hadley Falls Canal was soon plagued with problems, though. Local fishermen objected to the height of the dam, which, they said, obstructed the annual shad and salmon run to their spawning grounds. Farmers objected that flooding from the dam caused malaria outbreaks. The company finally removed the inclined plane and rebuilt a lower dam in 1800, but flooding between 1802 and 1823 washed out that dam and two replacements. Meanwhile, local

The Inclined Plane: Alternative to Locks

An ingeniously simple device for elevating an object up and over an obstacle, the inclined plane was a wheel-and-pulley arrangement that pulled or lowered loaded "cars" up or down a gently sloping "inclination" or slope, thus enabling them to climb or descend from one elevation to another.

The first inclined planes date back to at least 348 A.D. in China, where ox-powered capstans (like big spools) turned to wind or unwind the cables, hauling the boats out of the water, up the incline and down the other side.

In the case of the Hadley Falls Canal inclined plane, the face of the slope was stone, covered by heavy planking, and the "car" was a watertight box with folding gates at each end. Boats on the lower level floated directly into the car, its gates were closed, and, as the car was pulled up or let down, sluice gates emptied it of water. The 230-foot plane allowed cargo traveling on the canal to be lifted or lowered over an elevation of 53 feet.

On the Morris Canal, opened in New Jersey in 1831, water turbines were used to haul 25-ton boats in cradles over 23 single-track inclines, to a summit of 914 feet. Longer boats were sometimes hinged in the middle so they could more easily pass over the summits, and section boats—two separate boats joined together—were also introduced on the inclines.

On the Pennsylvania Main Line, a canal opened in 1834, section boats were divided up to travel in parts on railway trucks, or wheeled platforms, over the 37-mile Portage Railway. Then, once arrived at the end of the portage, they were reassembled to continue the rest of the voyage by water.

---

river traffic had begun to wane, and the South Hadley Falls Canal Company finally decided against rebuilding the dam and abandoned the canal.

Elsewhere up and down the Connecticut River, other canals were built and flourished. The longest and most important was the Windsor Locks Canal, providing a six-mile bypass around the Enfield Falls and rapids at Windsor, 12 miles upriver from Hartford. Still in use in the latter half of the 20th century—mostly for pleasure craft—it completely transformed the quiet life of those who lived along the Connecticut in the mid-1820s. As historian Stewart Holbrook once explained:

> What the Locks did was to bring all river traffic to a halt, briefly, and provide taverns on both sides of the river to cater to the captains and crews of the boats, to the passengers, and drovers, and the army of river drivers accompanying the rafts and booms of logs that were cut far up the river in Vermont and New Hampshire.

During these early years, though, New England's best-known canal was the Middlesex, built between 1794 and 1803 to connect Boston and Boston Harbor with the Merrimack River at Lowell, Massachusetts. It was constructed under the supervision of English canal builder William Weston. After 10 years of planning and digging, the completed Middlesex was over 27 miles long, with eight aqueducts and 50 stone and wood bridges. Its 20 locks, mostly of stone, raised boats to a summit of 107 feet above the tidewater at Boston and 27 feet above the Merrimack. The main water supply for the Middlesex came from the Concord River, with sluice gates opening into the canal where it crossed the river. Mules used a towpath floating on pontoons—a Middlesex Canal innovation—to pull boats across the river. To allow boat cross-traffic to move up- and down-river, the towpath was pulled aside. However, boats moving up and down the Concord often used the canal to bypass the falls at North Billerica, avoiding a bothersome portage. Boats up to 75 feet long traveled the canal, pulled, at least in the early days, by draft horses or oxen walking along the towpath next to the canal and hitched to the boats by a towline or rope. Boatmen at either end of the boat steered it away from the canal sides using paddles or poles.

Passengers aboard a packet boat approach Abbott's Landing in Woburn on the Middlesex Canal. With a driver mounted behind, horses, mules or oxen pulled the boats as they walked a towpath built alongside the canal. Middlesex Canal Association

Henry David Thoreau, who traveled a short stretch on the Middlesex in a small boat with his brother John in 1839, wrote this description in his journal, which later appeared in his first book, *A Week on the Concord and Merrimack Rivers*:

> We . . . left [the Concord River's] channel, just above the Billerica Falls, and entered the canal, which runs, or rather is conducted, six miles through the woods to the Merrimack, at Middlesex; and as we did not care to loiter in this part of our voyage, while one ran along the tow path drawing the boat by a cord, the other kept it off shore with a pole, so that we accomplished the entire distance in little more than an hour. This canal, which is the oldest in the country, and has an even more unique look beside the more modern railroads, is fed by the Concord, so that we were still floating on its water. . . .

As one historian notes with amusement, the Thoreau brothers, in their haste, violated several canal regulations in force at the time—among them the speed limit of four miles per hour!

The Middlesex Canal cost $528,000 to build, a very high sum for the time, and it operated for 50 years—from 1803 to 1853—with many financial ups and downs. In the end, the tolls (charged by the ton-mile—tons of cargo carried, multiplied by the number of miles traveled on canal waters), never compensated the shareholders for their investment. The canal's assets were finally ordered seized and forfeited on April 4, 1860, netting $130,000—which enabled the shareholders just barely to break even. But during

Lumber making its way through one of three sets of locks at Horn Pond on the Middlesex. Passage through took time, and packet boat passengers on the canal often whiled away the delays at one of the taverns like this one built along the banks. Middlesex Canal Association

Steersman guiding his barge through the lock gate at Horn Pond on the Middlesex, where the canal dropped 50 feet through three sets of double locks. Middlesex Canal Association

its heyday the Middlesex proved very useful. It provided access to, among other things, one of the country's earliest tourist resorts—complete with a restaurant, swimming, a picnic grove, band concerts, excursion boats and a bowling alley—at a place along its route called Horn Pond. At Middlesex Village, boats left the canal to move up the Merrimack River as far as Concord, New Hampshire—effectively opening up the interior of that state to commercial traffic. Down from New Hampshire came logs and timbers for shipyards in Medford. Granite for construction came down the canal from quarries at Westford and Tyngsborough. And much-needed goods from Boston made the return trip. In later years the canal supplied the textile mills at Lowell, Massachusetts with raw cotton and conveyed finished cloth from the mills to market. It was America's longest and most complex canal project prior to New York State's great Erie Canal.

Early American canal building was a learn-and-earn process. On-the-job training was the rule of the day, even for most of the chief engineers and construction bosses. Few Americans had even seen canals,

and fewer still had actually built them. Some books and papers about English canals were available in a few large libraries and some small private ones. But books weren't a substitute for experience or a good teacher when it came to the exacting job of actually building a canal. The occasional "expert," such as William Weston or John Christian Senf, was a rare find. For the most part Americans were on their own when it came to planning and construction. The work itself was what Americans today euphemistically call "labor intensive." Hundreds of workers toiled for countless hours—there were no great digging machines to get the job done. All 27-plus miles of the Middlesex were cleared and dug by hand with hundreds of men chopping and digging away with axes, picks and shovels. Blasting was done with crude black powder—such sophisticated explosives as dynamite and nitroglycerin had yet to be invented. Dirt and debris were moved or carried away by horse- or oxen-drawn wagons.

Little wonder that English and European visitors viewing the American canals expressed admiration

Historical Headlines

1607–1803

1607	First permanent English colony in North America is founded at Jamestown, Virginia.
1620	Pilgrims from England establish a colony at Plymouth, Massachusetts.
1624	New Amsterdam, later to become New York, is founded by the Dutch.
1634	St. Mary's City, first settlement in Maryland, is founded.
1677	Quakers settle in Burlington, New Jersey.
1681	William Penn founds the city of Philadelphia.
1683	Mennonites from Germany settle near Philadelphia, establishing a settlement called Germantown.
1729	Baltimore, Maryland is founded.
1732	Charter granted for an English colony in Georgia, last of the original 13 colonies to be settled.
1737	William Byrd founds the city of Richmond, Virginia.
1743	Benjamin Franklin establishes the American Philosophical Society to promote science in America.
1754	The French and Indian War begins, with Americans fighting on the side of the British against a French and Indian alliance. The war lasts until 1763.
1776	Congress adopts the Declaration of Independence, and the American Revolutionary War against England begins.
1783	American Revolution ends with Britain recognizing American independence.
1787	First American steamboat, invented by John Fitch, is launched on the Delaware River.
1789	Congress adopts the first 10 amendments (Bill of Rights) to the U.S. Constitution.
1793	Eli Whitney invents the cotton gin.
1803	Louisiana Purchase is negotiated with France, by which the United States acquires 828,000 square miles of territory for $15 million.
	Meriwether Lewis and William Clark begin their exploration of territory west of the Mississippi River.

for what the "unlearned" Americans had accomplished. But when some New Yorkers started talking about the next canal for their home state, a vast, 363-mile waterway connecting Albany to Buffalo, even many of their fellow countrymen grew skeptical that such a project could be completed.

3

BUILDING THE ERIE CANAL
1777–1825

Low bridge, everybody down.
Low bridge, for we are coming through a town.
And you will always know your neighbor,
You will always know your pal,
If you have ever navigated on
the E . . . R . . . I . . . E . . . canal!

—19th-century folk song

America was a growing nation in the early 1800s, and many Americans were restless. The roads were primitive, and the government quickly turned its attention to the nation's transportation needs. Many settlers, though, had already crossed the great Appalachian Mountain chain that separated the East from the West, carrying their belongings by hand or mule. Many had made their way to western New York, where clusters of small towns and villages had sprung up, and many, too, had moved even farther west along the bountiful regions of the Great Lakes.

The Appalachian Mountains virtually cut off these western pioneers from the rest of New York and the coastal cities. To make matters worse, from the government's point of view, because many of the Great Lakes villages and towns were not able to buy or sell goods in the East, they had established a lucrative trade with Canada to the north. Many New York merchants and politicians feared that, unless some link could be established with the western part of the state, the Great Lakes pioneers might annex themselves to Canada.

For many people, the most obvious way to link east and west was by water—the Hudson River already cut north from New York City past Albany and the east-west Mohawk River, flowing into the Hudson just north of Albany, stretched toward the Great Lakes. Some traffic was already flowing along these routes, but the journey was difficult, expensive and time consuming. New York City's harbor was broad and deep, and even large boats could easily navigate up the Hudson River through the peaceful valley east of the Catskill Mountains. But ship traffic came to a standstill at Albany, and cargo had to be unloaded and carried westward overland. The Mohawk River seemed to be the obvious route west from there, but unlike the

NEW YORK STATE
CANAL SYSTEM

Erie
Champlain
Cayuga-Seneca
Oswego

Map of the New York canals, including the Erie. Mid-Lakes Navigation Co. Ltd.

gentle and predictable Hudson, the Mohawk was a boatman's nightmare. Although some stretches along its westward ramble were peaceful, others contained wild, deadly rapids, sudden waterfalls and treacherous narrow passages spiked by dangerous rocks.

Still, the dream of connecting the two rivers into one, long navigable chain that would stretch from New York City to the Great Lakes had long persisted. Some enthusiasts had even tried to conquer the Mohawk by building a few small canals around its most difficult passages, notably several small locks around Little Falls between Schenectady and Utica. But most New Yorkers now realized that making the Mohawk a trouble-free waterway would be almost impossible. The link from New York City to the Great Lakes could parallel the Mohawk to make use of the route already cut by natural forces, but it would have to be an artificial one—a canal that would stretch 363 miles all the way from Albany to Buffalo.

It was a big dream, but not entirely a new one. Cadwallader Colden had hinted at it in 1724. And as early as 1777, Gouverneur Morris, a member of the First Continental Congress, had seen the need for just such a canal, and what it would bring to New York and the rest of the nation. "As yet, we only crawl along the outer shell of our country," he reasoned to his listeners, prophesying the day when a great New York inland waterway would connect the eastern coast with the Great Lakes.

Now as the financial and political potential of such a link began to be more fully realized, other New Yorkers were embracing Morris's dreams. In fact, the

state's lieutenant-governor, De Witt Clinton, became one of the idea's biggest supporters—once a political rival explained the benefits of the canal to him.

Some people, inside and outside the state, however, questioned both whether such a canal could be built and whether the project was financially sound. In 1809 even President Thomas Jefferson, usually a canal enthusiast, thought the idea impractical, calling such a canal "a splendid project" that might be constructed "a century hence," but adding that "it is a little short of madness to think of it at this day."

Undaunted, Morris and other New Yorkers had already begun to lay out plans when their schemes were interrupted by the War of 1812. Ironically, although the war was costly and made some New Yorkers wary about further heavy spending, the transportation problems that plagued U.S. troop movements also served to reinforce recognition of the need for the east-west link such an inland waterway would provide.

Before the war Morris headed a committee that had called for the canal to be constructed using a long inclined plane, something like the one at South Hadley Falls, though on a grander scale. Morris's plan called for an artificial slope that would incline gently all the way downhill from Lake Erie to Utica, providing just enough current to carry boats eastward, but not so much to make the going difficult for boats towed upstream against the flow. A closer look at finances after the war, though, revealed that building the long inclined plane would cost too much and would have to include a monstrous 150-foot-high aqueduct at one spot to keep the water running. Attempts to get financing for this scheme in England and France met with little interest, and the idea had to be abandoned.

The final plan, drawn up after the war, took a good look at the proposed canal route and its naturally gradual downward slope most of the way from Buffalo eastward. It called for a traditional canal, including 83 locks, 23 of those in the steep area between Schenectady and Albany. The artificial waterway would also need many bridges and aqueducts along its length. The estimated cost for the project was nearly $6 million and by the time it was finished actual cost would run over $7 million—a staggering amount for the day.

Miraculously, though, by promising that tolls along the canal would more than pay back the initial investment, the energetic De Witt Clinton, who now spearheaded the effort, was able to convince the wary New

York state legislature to part with the money. Construction began on July 4, 1817. It was a carefully selected date. Taxes would have to be raised to pay for the project, and Clinton and his canal supporters needed all the razzmatazz they could get to keep the public's spirits high on the whole idea. The ebullient spirit of Independence Day was sure to help.

BUILDING THE ERIE

Clinton picked the location for the ground-breaking ceremonies as carefully as he chose the date. The first earth was turned over at Rome, New York, approximately mid-way along the canal route. The area was comparatively level, and no major difficulties were expected for that portion of the waterway. Clinton wanted things to start as smoothly and efficiently as possible. Enough problems would crop up later on. The strategy was to keep the public's confidence up in the beginning.

Still, no one was fooled into thinking that the job was going to be an easy one. The plan called for over 360 miles of canal to be surveyed, planned, excavated

and built. No English or European canal that long had ever been constructed as a single project. Only a few longer ones existed anywhere and those had been constructed piecemeal, with gradual links between rivers, streams and lakes forged one by one until a long waterway gradually emerged.

The Erie Canal was to be 40 feet wide at the surface, gradually sloping downward to a width of 28 feet at the bottom. The actual waterway would be only four feet deep. Alongside the "ditch," a well-cleared towpath had to be constructed to allow mules, horses and oxen to pull the canal boats. Where necessary, locks, bridges and aqueducts would have to be built.

Three chief engineers were selected, each responsible for a different section of the project. James Geddes headed the western section from Buffalo to Seneca Lake; Benjamin Wright, the middle section from Seneca to Rome; and Charles Broadhead, the eastern section from Rome to Albany. Some thought that Broadhead had drawn the toughest job, for the eastern section included Little Falls and the summit link between Mohawk and Wood Creek. But each section had its own particular problems, and none of

The need for deep cuts through rocky ground like this, for locks on the west end of the Erie, and for more locks at the east end convinced canal planners that the place to start was in the middle, where the going was easier. Erie Canal Museum, Syracuse, New York

A broad towpath, carved out or built up along the canal, provided a route for teams of horses or mules using towlines to pull the boats.
Erie Canal Museum, Syracuse, New York

the three men was an experienced canal builder. Wright and Geddes were lawyers with some surveying experience, and they had traveled together to England to inspect the British canals. And Geddes had done much of the preliminary surveying of the entire Erie route. Beyond that, they had no experience. But then, almost no one in the country did.

For the work crews, Clinton encouraged his bosses to hire local farmers. He reasoned that the extra money to the locals would help keep support for the canal high. The problem was that local farmers also had their own crops and chores to attend to. Absenteeism ran high, and sometimes the men just walked off work in the middle of a job to take care of pressing farm matters. If the canal building was going to stay on schedule, something would have to change. The canal's hiring bosses sent recruiters to New York City, where thousands of hardworking Irish laborers were arriving each year. Fleeing from their impoverished homeland, the Irish were only too happy to be offered work. Wages were high—80 cents a day compared to an average wage of 80 cents a week in Ireland—and no questions were asked about a man's past or experience. Within months the canal was back on sched-

ule, and, as one newspaper reporter observed, it seemed that "every second man swore with a hearty Irish brogue."

The work began with surveyors marking out and staking the 60-foot path required for the canal and its towpath. Axemen then moved in to fell the trees, while other workers pulled the stumps and brush. Much of the land was a tangled wilderness, and the work was hard and slow. Working with mules and horses and without the benefits of modern machinery, laborers often needed as much ingenuity as muscle. One of the toughest and most time-consuming jobs was hacking through roots to free the stumps after trees had been felled. By tying a chain high up on a tree and fixing the other end to a wheel-and-gear device on the ground, one man winding the gear with a crank could pull over entire trees. The falling trees pulled their own roots free from the ground at the same time. For trees that had to be chopped down, leaving their stumps and roots behind, another device was invented that straddled the stump. Using mule power and an ingenious wheel-and-pulley arrangement, the machine pulled the stump free from the earth, roots and all.

Much of the work was still backbreaking, though, and there was much to learn about canal building and the obstacles produced by nature itself.

One part of the canal route ran through a long, dark section of woods called the Montezuma Marshes. The marshes were a dank, entangled swampland filled with thick and oozing black mud, snakes and mosquitoes. Fighting the mud that constantly seeped back into the newly dug channels was tough enough, but, to make matters worse, mosquitoes, many of them carrying malaria, attacked in force. They "fell upon the diggers in hordes," according to one source, and "the men came in with eyes swollen almost shut and hands so poisoned they could hardly wield tools." Through a long summer of digging, over 1,000 men fell violently ill with the fever. Many died. The situation was relieved only when the colder autumn nights brought an end to the mosquito attacks.

The marshes, consisting of nine miles of fluid mud, silt and cattails west of the Seneca River, presented engineering problems as well. When the workers tried to cut a channel through the muck, the walls oozed right back into the cut. So they had to dredge out the muck and then build up the banks with heavy earth hauled in from outside. Water seepage was also a problem on other parts of the newly dug ditches. Finally a young apprentice engineer named Canvass White found a nearby source of special limestone that, when used correctly, hardened under water. White quickly patented the process, and the limestone was used to seal the canal's walls.

Not all canal engineers and workers concentrated on clearing the land and digging the "ditch." Long "feeder" channels, complete with sluice gates, had to be dug to supply the canal with water. Drainage ditches had to be dug. Bridges had to be constructed to allow farmers to cross the canal with their livestock, and giant aqueducts had to be built to carry the canal itself across natural rivers and streams. All in all, more than 300 bridges, some large but most small, and some only seven feet above the water, were constructed along the route of the Erie Canal.

Even more impressive were the aqueducts. Basically bridges that carried water, the Erie aqueducts lifted the entire canal, waterway and towpath across nature's own rivers and streams. A few miles outside of Albany, the largest aqueduct, 1,182 feet long, spanned the Mohawk River itself, and at Rochester an imitation Roman-style aqueduct carried by nine 50-foot arches lifted the canal over the Genesee River.

Many other smaller aqueducts had to be constructed along the right-of-way.

Crossings—when the canal had to cross a stream or river—didn't always require an aqueduct though. Less difficult crossings were sometimes accomplished by damming the stream and allowing boats to just float across in the slack water behind the dam. A small bridge usually carried the towpath. The greatest engineering challenge faced by the enthusiastic but inexperienced Erie engineers was the construction of canal locks. None of them had ever built a lock before nor had they any formal training in the procedure. One of the most difficult sets of locks was assigned to another young surveyor-turned-engineer, Nathan Roberts. His problem was a steep, rock escarpment northeast of Buffalo that the canal would have to climb. Using only what knowledge he could glean from books, Roberts constructed a double set of five locks, one for eastbound and one for westbound traffic, that would carry traffic over a 66-foot variance in the canal's level.

Meanwhile, even as the work progressed, canal officials began to open sections of the finished canal for public use. The first section, which opened on October 22, 1819, was a 15-mile stretch running between Rome and Utica, New York. The first boat to travel its length made the trip in four hours—traveling just a little under four miles per hour. As other short sections were opened, the canal commission began collecting tolls to fund the project. Upstate New York had already begun to undergo a transformation, as described in a Utica newspaper:

Our village on Friday, twenty-fifth [of the current month], presented a scene of bustle and stir never before witnessed here. On Saturday the packet boat from Rochester left here with 84 passengers aboard on her first trip. A boat will leave this place every morning, Sundays excepted, during the season and continue through to the Genessee River.

By the winter of 1821, when ice brought canal traffic to a halt, 220 miles of canal sections had opened. Work had begun on the aqueducts across the Genesee and Mohawk Rivers, and many bridges had already been built. By the end of 1822, as many as 1,400 boats were traveling up and down the stretch between Rochester and Schenectady, carrying ham, bacon, flour, salt and other products from the western farms and returning with settlers eager to move west.

Why the Bridges Were Low

As the Erie Canal wound through the countryside, the waterway was dotted with hundreds of little bridges—80 between Little Falls and Schenectady alone. To win the approval of local farmers and residents who resisted the project, the commissioners had promised to provide crossings for cattle and pedestrians, for farm wagons and buggies, and they'd made good on their promises with these "occupation bridges." But they hadn't made them any bigger than absolutely necessary. As a result, many crossings left just enough clearance for a boat to pass under and no more—and so entered the helmsman's cry of "Low bree-g-e!" into canal lore.

Throughout the country, other canal builders followed suit so that the passengers were, as described by one traveler on the James River and Kanawha Canal, "compelled to squat very low to avoid being scraped off the deck. The situation was always ludicrous, and the accidents resulting from these low bridges, sometimes serious, but oftener absurd."

Charles Dickens, who chronicled his travels on the Pennsylvania Main Line Canal noted, too, "It was somewhat embarrassing at first, to have to duck nimbly every five minutes whenever the man at the helm cried, 'Bridge,' and sometimes, when the cry was 'Low Bridge,' to lie down nearly flat."

Passengers like these riding on the deck of a Middlesex Canal boat had to duck to avoid being swept into the water as their boat passed beneath bridges built for local farmers and merchants. Middlesex Canal Association

On the Erie Canal today, higher bridges and lift bridges like this one at Fairport, New York enable taller vessels—such as barges piled high with cargo—to navigate the canal system. Mid-Lakes Navigation Co., Ltd.

A double set of five locks stepped boats up the steep slope at Lockport, near Buffalo. Erie Canal Museum, Syracuse, New York

On October 26, 1825, nearly nine years after the first ground had been broken, the entire canal opened. The opening celebrations, according to reports, were the grandest that New York had ever seen. De Witt Clinton—by this time so closely associated with the canal, both politically and personally, that it was widely known as Clinton's Ditch—presided at the ceremonies. Elected governor of the state shortly before work began on the canal in 1817, Clinton had been forced out of office in 1823. But when his political opponents also removed him from the position of canal commissioner, voters who saw the career of Clinton and the future of the Erie as one reelected him shortly thereafter.

Now, aboard a canal packet called the *Seneca Chief,* Governor Clinton led a grand and colorful procession of boats down the entire length of the canal from Lake Erie to New York City. Aboard the *Seneca Chief* was a cask of Lake Erie water to be poured ceremoniously into New York Harbor. Under normal conditions, and without stops, the trip would take a little less than six days. But each town and village had a celebration planned along the way, and many were so raucous that

drunken crew members were continually being left behind and replaced.

In a memoir commemorating the festivities, Cadwallader D. Colden wrote, "The Aquatic display transcended all anticipations, twenty-nine steamboats, gorgeously dressed, with barges, ships, pilot-boats, canal-boats, and the boats of the Whitehall firemen, conveying thousands of ladies and gentlemen, presented a scene which can not be described. . . ."

Within a week after the opening ceremonies the Erie Canal was doing business full tilt. It was America's first major canal and at that time its greatest engineering success. Also, unlike many of the other canals that would follow, it was a tremendous financial success. By the end of 1825, tolls collected on the Erie amounted to $495,000, and 13,110 boats and rafts had traveled the short section between Albany and the junction at Watervliet about six miles up the canal. Within nine years after its opening ceremonies, the Erie had collected enough tolls to pay off its construction debts. It continued to make money for the state, over 10 times its construction costs, until tolls were finally abolished in 1882.

The Erie's success, though, far exceeded just the profits from the canal's operation. Eastern New York State now had its link with the west. By 1845 over 4,000 boats of various sizes and types operated on the Erie, plying traffic up and down its length, and the canal employed an estimated 25,000 men, women and children. The Erie Canal had become the nation's busiest "highway."

Western farmers who had once paid more than $100 a ton to ship their produce east now loaded it onto eastbound packets for only $10 a ton. Travel time had been cut by one-third. Moving westward, eastern goods and passengers flowed into what had once been a wilderness. Carnival boats, showboats, "traveling churches" and even "library boats" floated up the canal, along with the usual cargo and passenger boats, to serve the new towns and settlements.

Overnight, New York City became the nation's most important port. Buffalo, once a tiny village, became a rapidly growing major terminus, with more than 3,000 new houses constructed during the canal's first year of operation alone. By 1840 the city's population had mushroomed to over 18,000 people. Rochester, Syracuse and Utica became overnight boomtowns, and the city of Lockport, the site of Nathan Roberts's major engineering feat at the western end, quite literally sprang out of nowhere.

The Erie Canal served much more than just New York State. As a "road" across the Appalachians, it opened up another much-needed path to the Great Lakes and farther west. By 1840 travelers could make a trip from New York City to Cincinnati almost entirely by water—first up the Hudson River and along the Erie Canal, then by steamboat across Lake Erie to

To speed progress along the canal, some boats carried a change of horses. Here, a horse leaves the onboard stable to take its turn on the towpath. American Canal and Transportation Center

Along the Towpath of the Erie: Working on the Canal

Some 25,000 people were employed on the Erie Canal at its peak—men, women and children. The pay ranged from a high of $14 to $20 a month for boat captains to $8 to $14 a month for bowsmen (helpers) and $5 a month for drivers, or hoggees, who paced the horses or mules that towed the boats.

Along the canal, maintenance crews and locktenders kept things running smoothly. A towpath walker was responsible for each section of the canal, usually about 10 miles long, and would walk his section once a day, on the watch for trouble—accidents, leaks, floods, debris floating on the surface. The locktender, who manned the lock gates, worked night and day, responding to boat whistles of approaching craft, catching catnaps in between boats. He had a prime opportunity for earning extra money and usually capitalized on it, collecting tips and selling food, drink and goods to those who locked through or who tied up to wait their turn. Thousands of workmen stood by on call for repairs. They also cleared debris, removed sand bars and dredged the bottom, and rebuilt damaged towpaths and embankments—especially during the three months or more the Erie had to shut down for the winter.

Aboard the boats, the captain was king. Frederick Marryat, a retired British naval captain who traveled the Erie Canal in 1837 from Utica to Syracuse and then the Oswego Canal north to Oswego on Lake Ontario, gives us this impression of a canal boat captain's job:

> Set off for Oswego in a canal boat; it was called a packet boat because it did not carry merchandise, but was a very small affair, about fifty feet long by eight wide. The captain of her was, however, in his own opinion, no small affair; he puffed and swelled until he looked larger than his boat. This personage, as soon as we were under weigh, sat down in the narrow cabin, before a small table; sent for his writing desk, which was about the size of a street organ, and like himself, no small affair; ordered a bell to be rung in our ears to summon the passengers; and then, taking down the names of four or five people, received the enormous sum of ten dollars passage-money. He then locked his desk with a key large enough for a street-door, ordered his steward to remove it, and went on deck to walk just three feet and return again. After all, there is nothing like being a captain.

At the stern, the steerman handled the tiller to keep the boat, which was always pulled at an angle by the mules or horses on the towpath, from hitting the walls of the canal or other boats. Some boats would have two steersmen, one at each end, and a bowsman, or helper.

The hoggee, or driver, usually a young boy, ran along the towpath to pace and guide the team. He was responsible for keeping the towline from tangling—especially when boats were passing each other. According to the law of the canal, the faster packet boats had the right of way, while all other boats had to pull aside and lay their towlines slack to let them pass. A hoggee (the name probably came from the commands "Haw" and "Gee" that he yelled to his mules) who wasn't watchful in this situation would have to dive in after his team if they got dragged into the water by a tangled line.

Low on the totem pole was the cook, who spent all day in the tiny galley and whose efforts were rarely appreciated.

Cleveland, followed by another short canal trip to Portsmouth on the Ohio River and another short steamboat journey down the river to Cincinnati. Equally important, and almost forgotten in the light of the Erie's great success, was the fact that this canal served as a major training ground for men who would go on to help build the infrastructure of America. Many of these early American "engineers," who had

The Erie Canal at Lockport today. American Canal and Transportation Center

little or no formal training or experience before they worked on the Erie Canal, immediately moved on to other projects.

Benjamin Wright went on to become known as "the father of American engineering" by serving as chief engineer on the Chesapeake and Ohio Canal in 1828 and the St. Lawrence Canal in 1833. He served as a consulting engineer on many other North American canals, including the Welland, the Chesapeake and Delaware, and the Delaware and Hudson. Additionally, Wright surveyed railroad lines in New York, Illinois, Virginia and Cuba.

Nathan Roberts, who had been primarily a farmer before his work on the Erie locks, also served as a consulting engineer for the Chesapeake and Delaware Canal. He surveyed a ship canal around Niagara Falls, acted as chief engineer for the western section of the Pennsylvania State Canal, served on the board

of engineers for the Chesapeake and Ohio Canal Company and worked for the federal government as chief surveyor for a canal around Muscle Shoals, Alabama. In 1839 he returned to the Erie to help supervise a partial enlargement project to accommodate the canal's heavy traffic.

Canvass White, whose "waterproof limestone" discovery had helped in solving the Erie's seepage problems, went on to open a factory that produced cement by his patented process. He also superintended the construction of the Susquehanna and Schuylkill Canal, the New Haven and Farmington, the Lehigh, and the Delaware and Raritan.

John P. Jervis, a young lumber worker who had started out working on the canal as a simple axeman, rose to become an assistant to Benjamin Wright. He later succeeded Wright as chief engineer for the Delaware and Hudson Canal and Railroad. He designed

Erie Canal Facts

1777–1825

1777   Gouverneur Morris, member of the Constitutional Convention, first proposes a westward canal for New York.

1817   July 4. Work begins on the relatively easy middle sections. Surveyors James Geddes and Benjamin Wright learn by doing; Irish workers provide muscle, with 2,000 to 3,000 men working by December. Syracuse-to-Herkimer section is completed within a year.

         Engineer Canvass White goes to Europe to inspect canals and gain information.

1819   Rome-to-Utica section completed.

         A thousand workers die of malaria.

1820   As sections open, local economies boom. Utica-to-Rochester section completed; boat building thrives, trade flows, pioneers head west.

1822   "Clinton's Folly" falls under attack.

         The Erie Canal becomes a hot political issue and its completion is threatened; Clinton loses his bid for renomination for governor, leaving office in 1823, and is removed from the Canal Commission the following year.

1824   Rochester and Syracuse—seeing potential profits dwindling—go to bat for the canal. The partially finished canal already shows a profit, and Clinton is easily reelected governor.

1825   The *Seneca Chief* sails through.

         October 26. Amid jubilant celebration a fleet of boats cruises down the Erie Canal from Buffalo to New York City. The *Seneca Chief*, with De Witt Clinton aboard, heads the fleet.

---

braking devices for the inclined plane portages on the Allegheny Canal; was instrumental in bringing the first British railroad locomotive, the Stourbridge Lion, to the United States; and in 1831 served as chief engineer for the pioneering Mohawk and Hudson Railroad. In 1836 he planned New York City's Croton Aqueduct, and 10 years later he built a water supply system for the city of Boston. He also built bridges, short railroad lines and dams throughout New York and the Midwest.

William McAlpine, who at the age of 15 had been Jervis's apprentice on the Erie, became the canal's chief operating engineer for the eastern division in 1836. Later, after leaving the Erie, he designed water supply systems for Chicago, Brooklyn, Buffalo, Montreal, Philadelphia, San Francisco, New York and Toronto. McAlpine also supervised construction of the famous Erie Railroad as well as the Chicago and Galena, later called the Chicago and Northwestern Railroad.

He also worked as chief engineer for many bridges and in 1873 built the state capitol building at Albany, New York. As a park engineer in New York City, he planned Riverside Drive, and was in the middle of planning a New York subway system when he died in 1890 at the age of 75.

Many more Erie alumni, somewhat lesser known, went on to help construct roads, bridges, drainage and water supply systems, railroads, tunnels and dams throughout the United States.

As De Witt Clinton had promised, the Erie Canal paid back its debts. Its profit far exceeded what could be counted out in money. And the engineering vision, courage, imagination and skill used by those who built the Erie gave to the nation the promise of a new and growing future.

Historical Headlines

1804–1825

1804	Meriwether Lewis and William Clark set out to explore the territory west of the Mississippi River.
1807	Robert Fulton demonstrates his steamboat, the *Clermont*, on the Hudson River.
1810	Third U.S. census shows population at 7.2 million.
1811	The National Turnpike is begun.
1812	The United States declares war against Britain (War of 1812). The war lasts about two years.
1820	Congress passes the Missouri Compromise, prohibiting slavery in the Louisiana Territory north of the Mason-Dixon Line, latitude 36 degrees 30 minutes.
1824	America's first school of science and engineering opens, later called Rensselaer Polytechnic Institute.
1825	Erie Canal is completed in New York State.

4

THE BOOM DAYS
1825–1850

OHIO STARTS TO DIG

Even as New York State was completing the Erie Canal, the great canal boom had begun throughout the rest of the nation. As the Erie progressed, its opened sections moving heavy traffic and collecting tolls, other states watched its success and began to plan canals of their own.

Ohio, already benefiting from the western flow of settlers streaming along the Erie Canal and the more rugged overland routes, was quick to recognize the advantages of having a canal system of its own.

Although its land was fertile, and new farms were being settled quickly by the flow of new arrivals, most of the state's farms and towns were still struggling to survive. If Ohio was going to prosper, it had to be able to move its goods and produce to the large markets and bring more money in.

The success of the Erie had piqued the interest of Ohio citizens in canals, but the problem for the state legislature was how many canals the state could afford to build and along which routes. Every town and village, not too surprisingly, demanded to be included along a canal right-of-way.

In the interest of finding the best routes, James Geddes, who had worked on the Erie and Champlain canals, was asked to journey to Ohio in 1823 and make a preliminary survey. Geddes spent eight months and identified five possible canal routes. Money was still tight, though, and the whole question was put on hold

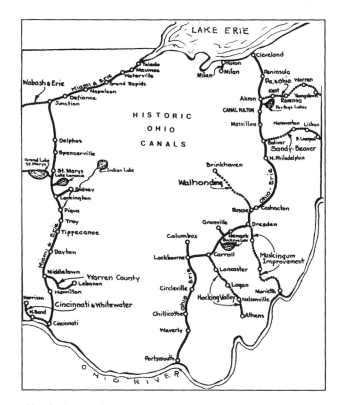

Ohio built the Miami and Erie and the Ohio and Erie to connect Lake Erie with ports on the Ohio River. American Canal and Transportation Center

until 1825, when the state legislature finally found enough financing to begin.

A new board of seven canal commissioners approved two separate canals along two different routes. The Ohio and Erie would run from the city of Cleveland on Lake Erie down to Portsmouth on the Ohio River, opening up Cleveland as a major port. The Miami, later called the Miami and Erie, was to run a shorter route, 66 miles from Cincinnati on the Ohio River to Dayton. Later an extension to Toledo and Lake Erie was added. To keep everybody happy, both canals meandered a bit along the way. The Ohio and Erie, in particular, was something of a rambler, stopping at many small towns that might have been bypassed if the planners had decided on a straighter, less expensive and decidedly less popular route.

On July 4, 1825, three months before the Erie Canal was officially completed, New York's De Witt Clinton was guest of honor at the ground-breaking ceremonies for Ohio's two proposed canals. Orator Thomas Ewing, waxing eloquent at the ceremonies, exclaimed euphorically: "See what my country has done in her juvenile state! And if she has achieved this gigantic enterprise in infancy, what will she not effect in the maturity of her strength, when her population becomes exuberant and her whole territory in full cultivation."

Work on the 66-mile-long Miami began first. To help the villages and towns along its route, some labor contracts for the digging were turned over to small local crews, but the bulk of Ohio's canal work was performed by the more experienced Irish laborers and bosses brought down from the Erie.

The 308-mile-long Ohio and Erie started shortly afterward. By autumn more than 2,000 laborers were at work on it. A sprawling main camp was set up at Cuyahoga Falls, and hundreds of wooden shanties and tents sprang up at the site, which later became the city of Akron.

The two canals were less complex than the Erie. To save money and labor (locks and aqueducts were time consuming and expensive), wherever possible much of the route was cut along existing streams. Most of the work involved simply clearing away trees and brush and cutting and lining "the ditches."

Saving money was a key part of the plan, and the source of many of the canals' problems. Despite the state's enthusiasm and support, the treasury was still meager. Payrolls were missed occasionally, and sometimes the chief engineers and labor bosses arrived at the sites not knowing if the work could go on or if it would be called to a halt by their superiors. Somehow, though, the digging continued.

Mosquitoes were an even bigger problem than they had been on the Erie. The Ohio summers were longer and warmer, and the decision to save money by using existing streams and marshlands exposed the workers to more hazards. Malaria killed hundreds of workers and made thousands of others sick. While the routes had been chosen so the work would go easier and thus be less expensive, the constant battle with mosquitoes and malaria along the right-of-ways slowed the work and increased the payrolls. The bad situation was not made any easier when hundreds of the original Irish bosses and workers quit their jobs to move to the new Pennsylvania canal projects and escape the "fever." In order to recruit replacements, wages had to be raised, putting more pressure on the state treasury.

Somehow, though, work continued and parts of the canals began opening to traffic as soon as they were finished. Ironically this, too, put pressure on the state's funds. Local merchants who had been selling cheaply to the canal contractors now began to ship their goods to other markets where they could get better prices. The contractors had to meet these higher prices to keep supplied.

The Ohio canals kept moving, crawling slowly across the state. Then, in 1832, work came to a halt when the cholera epidemic that had been sweeping across Europe arrived in America. This highly infectious disease had apparently arrived on ships docking in Quebec, Canada, with dying passengers aboard. Within weeks it had begun to spread down the Great Lakes. Much more deadly than malaria, cholera could strike anyone suddenly and without notice, killing within a matter of hours. Victims suffered profuse diarrhea, acute abdominal pain and severe dehydration. It traveled quickly and relentlessly, transmitted by contaminated water and often carried by the frightened people who were running away from it. The canals had opened up quick passages for travelers around the lakes—and the cholera followed them. In New York State, terrified citizens along the Erie Canal stopped traffic and burned incoming boats hoping to prevent the disease from entering their cities. The skies were darkened by the thick, black smoke from burning buckets of tar that the citizens incorrectly believed would "purify" the air.

Cholera hit Cleveland, Ohio in August 1832. Within weeks it had found its way to Cincinnati about 250 miles away on the Ohio River. Over 300 people

---

Canal Boom Facts

1792–1895

1792–1826 The Schuylkill Navigation Canal
The original canal was to run north from Philadelphia to Reading, Pennsylvania. The completed 108-mile waterway canalized the Schuylkill as far north as Port Carbon. Later it was connected to the Main Line Canal by the Union Canal.

1799, 1855 and 1895 The "Soo", or St. Mary's Falls Canals
Built between Lake Superior and Lake Huron on the St. Mary's River to get around the falls. Originally built on the Canadian side in 1799, destroyed in the War of 1812, rebuilt in Michigan in 1855 and in Canada in 1895.

1817 Champlain, or Northern, Canal
Opened up transportation for rich mineral and timber resources in the Adirondack Mountains in New York. It ran from Fort Edward, the upper limit of navigation on the Hudson River, to Whitehall, at the southern tip of Lake Champlain.

1821–28 The Union Canal
Built to connect Reading and Middletown, Pennsylvania, it was originally begun in 1792. Not used as part of the Main Canal system, however, because of its small locks, narrow channel, and inadequate water supply. Bypassed by the Columbia-Philadelphia Railroad in 1834.

1825–33 Ohio and Erie Canal
Opened up Cleveland on Lake Erie to Ohio River traffic from Portsmouth, Ohio, enabling Erie Canal traffic from as far away as New York to route across the state of Ohio.

1825–45 Miami and Erie Canal
Connected the Ohio River port of Cincinnati to the port of Toledo on Lake Erie.

1826–29 Oswego Canal
Built to connect the Erie Canal at Syracuse, New York to Oswego, New York on Lake Ontario.

1826–34 The Pennsylvania Canal
Also known as the "Main Line Canal," it ran between Philadelphia and Pittsburgh, with a horse-drawn railroad running from Philadelphia to Columbia and a portage railroad over the Allegheny Mountains.

---

died within days along the Ohio and Erie route and the Ohio River. Work along the canals was stopped immediately, and the opened sections were closed in an effort to stop the spread of the disease. The reduced number of travelers and the winter freeze ended the worst of the epidemic, although it continued in a milder form throughout the next few summers. By 1833, with the worst over and the canals and roads opened once again, more travelers now arrived in Ohio than ever before. The westward migration had picked up as families fled the East in hopes of finding a safer, cholera-free haven in the pure air of the West.

On January 22, 1833, after eight long years of construction, both Ohio canals were officially opened. Although the promised extension of the Miami Canal to the Maumee River and Lake Erie wasn't completed until 1845, Ohio's canals were a tremendous success. The state's population swelled as many of the canal travelers settled in, taking advantage of the available open spaces and fertile land. Commerce and goods flowed in a steady stream along the northern and southern routes of the canals, soon bringing more money to the state treasury and the pockets of its citizens. Akron, Newark and Chillicothe became major trade centers, and Ohio itself soon became the third most populous state in the Union.

Once extended along the full route from the Ohio River to the lake port of Toledo, the Miami and Erie Canal became one of the most profitable and long-lived canals in the country. In its first full year of operation it brought $233,527 into the state coffers. In 1903, despite competition from the railroads and long after most other canals had grown over with weeds, its tolls still came to more than $70,000.

Meanwhile, east of Ohio, another canal system had been waging it own struggle for success.

PENNSYLVANIA BUILDS ITS "GRAND CANAL"

Pennsylvanians, disturbed that the Erie Canal had made nearby New York City a greater port than Philadelphia, planned a canal that would compete directly with that of the rival New Yorkers. The problem was that, unlike New York, whose canal followed the route of the Mohawk River, Pennsylvania had no natural break through the Appalachians. Undaunted, the citizens demanded that their canal stretch all the way from Philadelphia across the state to Pittsburgh. They left figuring just how to proceed to the engi-

Canal boats traveling on the Ohio canals in 1904. American Canal and Transportation Center

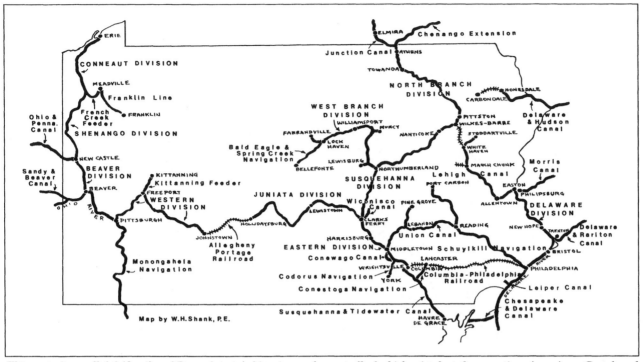

This map shows all 1,243 miles of Pennsylvania's historic canals—not all of which existed at the same time. American Canal and Transportation Center

neers. To make sure that the job would be done right, they even imported a team of the Erie's prime problem solvers. Shortly after the state legislature authorized a go-ahead on February 25, 1825, James Geddes was lured away from his work on Ohio's canals by the Pennsylvania project. Two of his Erie co-workers, Nathan Roberts and Canvass White, also joined him in Pennsylvania.

With crews of Irish and German workers arriving on the scene, too, ground was broken at Harrisburg alongside the Susquehanna River on July 4, 1826, and the strange route of the Pennsylvania Canal was ceremoniously begun.

Opening in 1834, nine years after the Erie, the Pennsylvania Canal was soon one of the most talked about in the nation. What Geddes and the Pennsylvania Canal engineers had planned was a unique and complex system that had as many people shaking their heads in disbelief as in wonder.

Travelers from Philadelphia, wishing to visit relatives in Pittsburgh by way of the new canal system, would pack their bags early and board not a boat but a "State Railroad Coach." Drawn by horses as its wheels moved along the tracks, the "railroad coach" would proceed slowly from Philadelphia until it reached the first steep hill. There, the horses were unhitched and

the coach was hooked onto a cable that would pull it up the tracks to the crest of the hill. Once at the top travelers would wait until the cable was unhooked and a fresh team of horses hitched. Then they would be on their way again, moving by rail down the narrow track another 75 miles or so until they reached Columbia. At Columbia, weary after the 20-hour journey from Philadelphia, they would be shifted to a canal boat. This boat would travel alongside the Susquehanna River, through 14 locks for 43 miles until it reached a tiny artificial lake created by a high dam where the Juniata River flowed into the Susquehanna. There travelers would find themselves and the boat being towed, still traveling on canal water, through a series of aqueducts, across the artificial lake and the Juniata River. After passing through another 88 locks to achieve a rise of 584 feet, the canal boat would then continue another 127 miles on to Hollidaysburg, Pennsylvania, where at last travelers could disembark for the night and try to get some rest before the next leg of the journey.

The rest was sorely needed. As dawn broke the next morning, travelers would pick up their bags again and board another horse-drawn railway. After four slow miles (traveling at six miles an hour) and enough time to shake the sleep from their eyes, weary voyagers

Not designed for people in a hurry, traveling along canals often involved delays, resulting in long lines of canal boats like these stuck waiting for repairs along the North Branch of Pennsylvania's Susquehanna Canal. American Canal and Transportation Center

would suddenly find themselves at the most talked about part of the Pennsylvania Canal system.

To get passengers and cars over the crest of the steep Allegheny Mountains separating Hollidaysburg from Johnstown, Canvass White had built the famous "Allegheny Portage Railroad."

If the gentle rocking of the coach had tempted travelers to return to sleep, the Portage Railway was quick to open their eyes again. Watching the horses being unhitched once more and the coach being attached to another cable, travelers were suddenly confronted with the fact that they were now going to be pulled up the tracks for a total climb of over 1,000 feet. The motor-driven cables would pull the coach up the first of five steep slopes. At the top, the coach would switch once again to natural horsepower, to be pulled a few miles to the beginning of the next climb. There it would be attached to yet another cable, pulled steeply upward along the tracks, unhooked, and hitched up to horses again. The process would be repeated three more times until the summit of the

mountain was reached. There exhausted travelers would disembark for the night. Then, after a quick breakfast, they would board the car and repeat the entire process as the coach was let down the opposite side of the mountain. If travelers still had breakfast in their stomachs by the time they reached bottom, they could enjoy the experience of having the coach pulled through the longest tunnel then in America, 901 feet of semidarkness, finally emerging from the six-hour, 37-mile portage at Johnstown. Here they would board another canal boat to begin the concluding leg of their journey through a 105-mile section of canals, including another series of locks—and on at last to Pittsburgh.

Although slow and fatiguing, the trip certainly was a colorful experience—doubtless a good conversation starter upon arrival and for years to come. Even the English novelist Charles Dickens was enthralled by the Pennsylvania Canal.

Unfortunately, even though the fast packets made the trip in six days—competitive with the Erie Canal—

Historical Headlines

1826–1850

1829   The world's oldest railroad bridge, the Carrollton Viaduct, is built by the B&O Railroad at Gwynn's Falls near Baltimore, Maryland.

1830   U.S. census counts 12.8 million people in the United States 150,000 immigrants have arrived since 1820.

1834   Cyrus McCormick of Virginia patents first successful mechanical reaper.

1836   Texas becomes a republic independent from Mexico; Samuel Houston is president.

1840   Sixth national census shows the U.S. population has swelled to 17 million, with 600,000 immigrants arriving between 1830 and 1840.

         William Howe patents a new, stronger truss design for bridges, incorporating iron rods.

1842   John Frémont explores Oregon-bound route west of the Mississippi, as far as South Pass in Wyoming.

1844   The United States negotiates annexation with Texas.

1846   Mexican War (resulting from U.S. annexation of Texas) begins.

1848   Gold discovered at John Sutter's camp in California, setting off the Great Gold rush of 1849 the following year.

         Treaty ends Mexican War. Mexico cedes to the United States what is now California, Arizona, Nevada, Utah and parts of New Mexico, Colorado and Wyoming in exchange for payments by the U.S. government.

1850   Bitter debates in Congress over slavery result in the Compromise of 1850, admitting California as a free state (the 31st state) and allowing new territories of New Mexico and Utah to decide the slavery issue for themselves.

         Overland mail delivery is established for the first time west of the Missouri River, from Independence, Missouri to Ogden, Utah.

---

times had already begun to change. Businessmen in a hurry and farmers and traders shipping freight were not very happy with the time or the expense involved in traveling Pennsylvania's new canal. Branches were gradually added, forking into the "Main" or "Grand" Canal as it had come to be called, but the Pennsylvania system was not a financial success. Its operational costs were much too high and it could never pay off its initial debts.

5

CONSTRUCTION CONTINUES:
A LOSING RACE WITH THE IRON HORSE
1825–1840

"Those ain't canals, boys," one self-assured railroad builder remarked to news reporters in the early days of the railroad locomotive. "They're just big drainage ditches that the money washes away in!"

During the boom days of American canals, before the steam-driven locomotive changed the nation forever, these "ditches" were America's most efficient highways.

The boom days of the canal were not to last, however. Even as many of the later "ditches" were being dug, tracks were being laid for the pioneering steam locomotives.

In South Carolina in 1830, the Best Friend of Charleston, one of the nation's first locomotives, began to carry passenger coaches on a regular run. A few progressive canal companies, such as the enormously profitable Delaware and Hudson, chartered in 1825 to carry coal between the Delaware and Hudson rivers, had begun to experiment with steam locomotives, and some young American civil engineers were even engaging in fantastic talk about the day when trails of cross ties and rails would crisscross the continent.

ACTION ALONG THE DELAWARE

For a time, though, the canal business continued to thrive. The Erie Canal, the Ohio canals and the Penn-sylvania system were state owned and financed. Along the Middle Atlantic coast, many short, privately financed canals were also being built—often to carry coal. The Delaware and Hudson Canal (for which Brooklyn Bridge designer John A. Roebling built an aqueduct, learning the craft he would use on his masterpiece) had been privately financed; so had the Lehigh Canal.

Begun in 1825 to carry anthracite from the coal fields at Mauch Chunk, Pennsylvania along the Lehigh River down to Easton, Pennsylvania on the Delaware River, the Lehigh Canal survived well into the railroad era. Its success was due in part to the foresight of its developer and first chief engineer, Josiah White. A successful and tenacious businessman, White had purchased a coal field at Mauch Chunk and planned his canal to transport the hard, black fuel to the booming coastal market.

Despite the skepticism of his less imaginative business associates, White built his canal not only for his present needs but for the future as well. Although the Lehigh Canal was relatively short, comprised of only 46 miles of actual canal and 10 miles of slack, or slowly flowing water, it was big. Running through stone locks 100 feet long, the canal was 60 feet wide at the top and tapered down to 40 feet wide at the bottom. It was also five feet deep, a foot deeper than the Erie. Wide and

On the Lehigh Canal north of Allentown in 1925. American Canal and Transportation Center

deep enough, White reasoned to handle larger boats in the future.

Ground was broken in April 1825. After getting his project started, White turned the job of chief engineer over to the more experienced canal builder Canvass White (no relation to Josiah), who had worked on the Erie. The Lehigh was finished in June 1829 and went into full operation a month later. It was an immediate success, carrying over three-quarters of a million tons of coal a year during its lifetime. As described in 1912 by W. H. Gausler, who ran his own boats on the canal from 1840 to 1856, traffic along the Lehigh ran on a 24-hour, seven-day-week schedule to keep up with the heavy demand, from thaw until the water iced over each year:

Up to 1843 the boats ran on Sunday, the canal being the only means to bring freight to Philadelphia. Boating was carried on from the first of April to December. Nearly all boatmen kept going day and night, boats being so numerous that the canal seemed to be a solid mass of boats. The different coal operators offered premiums for one year to the boat that brought the most coal to Philadelphia. This was contested by about four boats, myself being one of them. We never tied our boats, nor stopped day or night during the boating season; this was done to get as much coal to market during the eight months of boating as possible.

Not even the railroads could put the bustling Lehigh out of business. It continued to carry traffic well into the 20th century.

The Lehigh had been built so well, in fact, that it was to become a link-up point for other short canal systems.

The Morris Canal, begun in 1831, ran between the Lehigh at the Delaware River and New York Harbor. Its builders planned to tap into the rich coal regions accessed by the Lehigh and trade with the New York area. The Morris, however, was built shallow and narrow and was barely able to carry traffic in its day, let alone meet the heavy demands of the future. Unlike the Lehigh Canal, with the coming of the railroads, the Morris vanished quickly.

The Delaware Division Canal of the Pennsylvania canal system started at Easton and cut 60 miles down the Delaware River to Bristol, Pennsylvania. Beginning in 1854, when the Delaware Divisions outlet lock at New Hope was constructed, coal traffic could pull out of the Lehigh Canal and cross the Delaware River from the Pennsylvania side. Then the loads of Lehigh anthracite could connect with the feeder canal of the Delaware and Raritan Canal on the New Jersey side, and from there continue down the Delaware and Raritan across New Jersey to New York Harbor. The connection turned out to be handy for the Lehigh and profitable for everyone.

New Jersey's busy Delaware and Raritan, though, was much more than a coal route conveniently used by Lehigh coal traffic. Supervised by the hard-working Canvass White, who seemed to be everywhere that a canal was being dug in those days, the canal was begun in 1830 and finished in 1834. It connected two of the nation's largest and most important cities: Philadelphia and New York. Despite heavy opposition from freight wagon companies that had been plying the route, the canal was popular immediately. Later, when the D & R pooled its interests with the pioneering little Camden and Amboy Railroad, which was chartered the same year, the two companies held an almost complete monopoly in freight traffic between the two cities, driving the wagon companies into bankruptcy before themselves falling in the 1870s under the pressure of the great Pennsylvania Railroad.

THE CHESAPEAKE CONNECTION

A little farther south the canal business was also booming around the busy Chesapeake Bay area.

As far back as 1786, the ever-inventive Benjamin Franklin had proposed building a canal that would slice across the narrow strip of land separating the

The inclined plane at Newark on the Morris Canal. American Canal and Transportation Center

Chesapeake Bay from the Delaware Bay. It seemed a logical idea, given the proximity of the two bays, and one that would make up for nature's failure to make the connection. Both money and experience were in short supply, however, and the Chesapeake and Delaware Canal was not actually begun until the Erie Canal proved how successful a canal could be.

The new planners' first thought was to hire Benjamin Wright away from his job on the Erie, but for reasons of his own Wright declined and the commission to build the canal was turned over to John Randle, Jr.

Randle was relatively inexperienced—although he scouted out a more viable route than the original plan called for, he overlooked the need for dams to provide water for the canal (three were required), and he completely underestimated the difficulty of the cut through the peninsula's backbone. Still, what he lacked in knowledge, he made up for in hard-driving determination, and the Deep Cut, as it was called, became known as one of the great engineering feats of his time. Nature had not supplied

---

The Crest and Decline of the Canal Era

1826–1860

1818–29 Lehigh Canal
Built by coal entrepreneur Josiah White, this successful canal connected Mauch Chunk, in the Pennsylvania coal fields, with Easton, Pennsylvania on the Delaware River. In 1832, when the Delaware Division Canal was completed, boats on the Lehigh could reach Philadelphia.

1824–31 Morris Canal
Built to cross New Jersey to Newark Bay from Phillipsburg, Pennsylvania, connecting with the Lehigh Canal terminus across the Delaware River. This was the "highest climbing" of the early canals, using inclined planes instead of locks to overcome a total rise and fall of 1,674 feet.

1825–28 Delaware and Hudson Canal
Improved from 1842 to 1850, with an aqueduct built by John A. Roebling, builder of the Brooklyn Bridge.

1828–60 Chesapeake and Ohio Canal
Originally the Patowmack Canal, planned by George Washington to connect Chesapeake Bay with the Ohio River via the Potomac River. Resumed as a joint project of the federal government, Virginia and Maryland in 1828, the C & O was completed from Georgetown, Delaware to Cumberland, Maryland. Construction halted in 1860, never reaching the Ohio.

1830–34 Delaware and Raritan Canal
Built to connect the two great ports of Philadelphia and New York, running from Philadelphia through Port Jervis to Kingston, New York on the Hudson River.

1832–58 James River and Kanawha Canal
Canal in Virginia envisioned by George Washington to connect the coastal tidelands at Richmond with the Ohio River in the West by connecting the James River with the Kanawha in what is now West Virginia. Begun in 1790 as the James River Canal, only a few locks were completed. Work resumed in full force in 1832. By 1851 the canal extended as far upriver as Buchanan, 196½ miles from Richmond. The James River and Kanawha Company bought out North River Navigation in 1858, extending its canal service as far as Lexington, but beyond that point no further construction was ever completed.

---

such a connection for a good reason. The ground was composed of solid granite, and at places it almost completely resisted penetration by the workers' primitive tools.

To slice through one area of almost solid granite, Randle had employed a small army of nearly 2,500 men using hand tools. Dangerous black powder was used for blasting, and many of the men were maimed or killed in rock slides and explosions. In some places the cut was 90 feet deep and over 60 feet wide. The monetary cost of just hauling away the rocks and debris was disheartening and at times almost became a separate major project itself.

The 13-mile canal was finished and opened to traffic by October 17, 1829. But the total cost was staggering for a canal so short: more than $2 million. Mile for mile it was the most expensive canal project in the nation. But once finished, the Chesapeake and Delaware Canal also became one of the most important and heavily traveled in the nation.

Taking advantage of the cut between the two major bays, another canal, the Susquehanna and Tidewater, was built between 1836 and 1839. Stretching for 43 miles between Havre de Grace in Maryland and Wrightsville, Pennsylvania, across from Columbia on the Susquehanna River, it funneled part of its traffic through the Chesapeake and Delaware and on up to Philadelphia while the rest continued down the Chesapeake to Baltimore. The Susquehanna and Tidewater traffic helped boost the revenue for the Chesapeake and Delaware, but not enough—the construction costs had badly burdened that canal financially. In 1870 the Reading Railroad bought out the Susquehanna and Tidewater Canal—locks, stock and whatever barrels it had lying around. And in 1919 the U.S. government purchased the floundering Chesapeake and Delaware Canal and all its assets, widening and deepening it enough to accept larger oceangoing ships. It is still in operation today, a valuable link for Chesapeake Bay shipping.

In the late 1820s hopes were still high for the connections and profits canals could bring, though, and along the Chesapeake, as elsewhere in the nation, great plans were still being made.

The success of the Erie Canal also brought back to life two of George Washington's dreams for major east-west canal links: An extension of the Patowmack Canal to stretch all the way to the Ohio River, via the Potomac, from what by now was Washington, D.C.; and, farther south, the James River and Kanawha

Guiding an excursion boat through a rebuilt lock on the Chesapeake and Ohio Canal in the 1980s. American Canal and Transportation Center

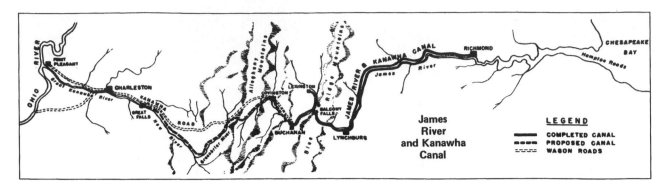

The James River and Kanawha Canal, as planned, never reached completion. American Canal and Transportation Center

Canal, begun in 1790 to connect Richmond, Virginia with the Kanawha, which flows into the Ohio River in what is now West Virginia.

For the northern of these two plans Washington had proposed a series of canal and lock connections that would allow boats to travel from the Chesapeake Bay up the Potomac River to Georgetown and then on to Cumberland, Maryland and farther west to the Ohio River.

With the Erie Canal opening up a northern route to the Ohio River, this plan began to gain appeal for the citizens of Virginia and Maryland, who were now calling for a connection of their own. After conducting what would today be called a "feasibility study," a joint project involving Virginia, Maryland and the federal government was organized and Benjamin Wright was hired as chief engineer. For further insurance, the Erie's Nathan Roberts was added to the canal's consulting board of engineers. Work on the Chesapeake and Ohio Canal began in 1828.

Ironically, though, Washington's dreams, which had been too ambitious to see completion during his lifetime, were outdated by the mid-1800s. In 1850, after 185 miles of the canal had been completed and put into use between the city of Washington and Cumberland, work came to an abrupt stop. Before it could be picked up again, the Baltimore and Ohio Railroad had established the connection—and no more picks and shovels were ever again turned on the Chesapeake and Ohio Canal. Today, like many other early canals, the Chesapeake and Ohio is designated as a national historic park.

Meanwhile the spark had not died on Washington's other dream—a James River and Kanawha connection. In Washington's time, a few small improvements along the James River—locks to circum-

vent rapids and falls—had made navigation easier. But little else of his plan had seen completion. Now, in the 1830s, over 40 years after the original plan had been proposed, work began once again on the James River and Kanawha Canal. Again Benjamin Wright was put in charge, and by 1837 over 3,000 slave laborers had begun digging the great east-west channel. But Virginia's canal dreams seemed destined always for failure. The James River and Kanawha fought financial problems every inch of the way. By the time it successfully opened a stretch 146 miles long from Richmond to Lynchburg, still far short of connecting with the Kanawha, most people felt that only a miracle had gotten it that far. The determined builders continued, pushing on to Buchanan, Virginia by 1851. But, like the ill-fated Chesapeake and Ohio, the James River and Kanawha Canal also fell far short of its intended connections. In 1859 a railroad line opened in competition from the city of Washington to Lynchburg, forcing the canal operators to reduce their tolls. Even the packet passengers seemed less than enchanted, as indicated by one who, after taking a trip in 1864, described the James River and Kanawha Canal as "a ditch filled with slimy water, snakes, and bullfrogs." At journey's end, the writer says, "Groping our way, by the aid of a feeble lantern, along a narrow footway on the top of the great arch where a stream passed under the canal, and gaining at last the open ground, we felt the infinite relief one always experiences upon reaching terra firma after a perilous voyage by water."

Floods and the Civil War played havoc with the canal, and its original records were destroyed when Richmond was burned in 1865. In 1877 the end finally came for the last of George Washington's canal dreams when a flood destroyed most of the still- un-

Night Travel on the James River and Kanawha Canal

While travel by packet boat was smooth and leisurely, travelers still looked upon even a short voyage as an adventure. Little wonder, given the accommodations they had. Freight and baggage were piled on deck, but only a small, stuffy compartment was provided inside. As a result, many people preferred riding out on the crowded deck, as one traveler on the James River and Kanawha Canal explains in a rare description of a trip in 1864: "The young folk and the soldiers, of whom there were a number on board, contented themselves until darkness came on, with seats upon the trunks, bags, and barrels upon the deck, passing away the time in conversation, or in watching the every-varying landscape."

Inside, the writer tells us, the boat was

a shell divided into four main compartments. The forward and largest compartment was for passengers; behind it was the kitchen, then a compartment for servants, and lastly, the captain's room in the stern. The passengers' cabin was divided by a curtain drawn across it forward, beyond which, extending into the bows, was the ladies' compartment. Where people were to sleep in such a place was the first problem presented upon entering the cabin. It was an open space, with nothing but long benches or lockers on either side, a table running down the center, a stove, and a few primitive stools. On either side of the boat were many windows. When the sleeping berths were adjusted, as hereafter described, they varied in desirability, according to their location with reference to the floor or the red-hot stove."

Although the packet left Richmond at five o'clock in the afternoon and completed the 20-mile trip at ten-thirty that same evening, with little else to do after darkness fell, the passengers spent part of the trip sleeping—or trying to—in a thicket of canvas hammocks hung one above the other inside the compartment. "At bedtime," the author tells us,

stout leather straps were produced and hooked to the ceiling and the floor. Between these, by ingenious arrangements, were stretched at intervals canvass hammocks. From the lockers under the benches on each side, beds and bed-clothing were produced and placed upon the hammocks and the tables. By the time the beds were down there was scarcely space for any one to turn himself around between them.

The James River and Kanawha Canal packet office in Richmond, Virginia in 1865. Virginia State Library

By day, low bridges often swept unwary passengers into the murky water, women's hoops ballooning out comically to buoy them up. By night, the crowded conditions made for short tempers and, no doubt, frequent attacks of claustrophobia. But finally, the boat would arrive, and the trip would begin to take on the nostalgic proportions of a conversation piece: "And so, after we had passed Walker's bridge and Stanard's low-bridge, the last horn blew for us; the tow-line slacked; the fiery steeds stood panting on the tow-path, and the boat sidled proudly up to the granite coping of Dover Mills, our destination."

Historical Headlines

1851–1869

1853   The United States purchases areas now located in Arizona and New Mexico for $10 million, adding the last territories currently forming the contiguous United States.

1854   The Republican Party is founded, championing, among other causes, the call for a transcontinental railroad.

1855   Pro-slavery and abolitionist factions battle in Kansas until peace is restored by federal troops in 1856.

1857   The Dred Scott Decision by the U.S. Supreme Court declares the Missouri Compromise unconstitutional and holds that living in a free territory does not make a slave free.

1860   Abraham Lincoln is elected President.

South Carolina secedes from the Union, joined in 1861 by Mississippi, Florida, Alabama, Georgia, Louisiana, Texas, Virginia, Arkansas, North Carolina and Tennessee, when these 11 states form the Confederate States of America.

1861   April 12. Confederates fire on Fort Sumter, Charleston, South Carolina and the Civil War begins. It lasts five years, until 1865.

Kansas becomes the 34th state; West Virginia breaks away from Virginia and becomes the 35th state in 1863.

1864   Lincoln is reelected President.

1865   The Civil War ends; over the next few years the secessionist states are readmitted to the Union.

Lincoln is shot and killed by John Wilkes Booth; Vice President Andrew Johnson becomes president.

13th Amendment to the Constitution abolishing slavery is ratified by 27 states.

1867   Albert Fink builds a truss railroad bridge across the Ohio River to Louisville, Kentucky.

The United States buys Alaska from Russia for $7.2 million.

1869   May 10. The first transcontinental railroad is completed with a ceremony at Promontory Point, Utah.

Wyoming Territory gives women the right to vote.

---

finished James River and Kanawha. The Richmond and Allegheny Railroad quietly bought up what was left of the canal and its assets, and put the James River and Kanawha Canal out of business.

BEGINNING OF THE END

On July 4, 1828, in Georgetown, Maryland, President John Quincy Adams dug the first spadeful of dirt to begin construction of the Chesapeake and Ohio. The fact that it took the president three tries to get his shovel into the ground may have held an omen for the future, not only for that canal, but also for others throughout the country. For on that same day, in the city of Baltimore another transportation network was born in the United States: the Baltimore and Ohio Railroad.

Most people didn't realize it at the time—for canal fever was still in full swing in 1828—but that was the beginning of the end. Railroads could run all winter long; canals could run only when the water wasn't frozen. Railroads were easy and inexpensive to build; canals were costly engineering projects. And, as railroads began to use bigger and faster steam locomotives, trains became faster and faster; canal boats were generally slow and inefficient.

In New York, the Mohawk and Hudson Railroad began building tracks parallel to the Erie Canal and inaugurated service in 1831. In Pennsylvania, the Pennsylvania Railroad was established in 1846 and soon began stretching its lines out across the state. In 1857 the Main Line Canal, unable to hold up against the competition, capitulated, giving over the entire Philadelphia-Pittsburgh portion of its route over to the Pennsylvania Railroad. And in Virginia, railroad tracks were completed between Richmond and Lynchburg in 1859, enabling passengers to make a trip to Lexington by rail and packet in 24 hours—20 hours less than on the James River and Kanawha Canal. Up and down the coast the story was the same.

At first the canals tried to hold the railroads down. They fought against railroad charters and lobbied for legislation to restrict railroad operation to the five months of the year when the canals had to close. And they reduced their tolls. But it became harder and harder for them to make a profit as one by one the railroads duplicated their routes with faster, more efficient transportation. And soon the canals were transporting supplies for the track layers and letting the railroads use their lines as feeders.

Not everyone was ready to give up, though. As late as the 1850s, canal fever still hadn't died down in at least two states in the Midwest, Indiana and Illinois.

6

CANALS COME TO THE MIDWEST— ALL BUT TOO LATE: INDIANA AND ILLINOIS

Although the economic success of the Erie had provided the inspiration for the great canal boom that swept the nation, not everyone in New York State had shared in that success. One inevitable aspect of the canal's prosperity was that land prices shot sky high along its banks, as well as in other parts of the state with access to the canal. Land that once was valued at a few hundred dollars jumped almost overnight into the thousands, beyond the means of many prospective buyers—who were mostly small farmers and business owners. While many people with financial backing or substantial funds of their own were able to reap the rich Erie harvest, others could no longer dream of settling in the booming area. And the same story was happening along the nation's other newly opened canals.

As a result, more and more farmers and entrepreneurs joined the trek west, looking for land that they could afford and opportunities they could develop. Joined by those hoping to escape the threat of cholera, this westward rush pushed first on to Ohio and then began to filter farther west to the even less densely populated states of Indiana and Illinois.

INDIANA'S BOOM BUSTS (1832–1852)

Like its neighbor state of Ohio, in the 1830s Indiana was both poor and unhappy with its condition. Also like Ohio, it looked with envy on the Erie Canal. Actually, Indiana developers had been flirting with the idea of canals for a long time. As far back as 1805, the controversial politician Aaron Burr had been part of a proposed canal enterprise, a two-mile "ditch" around Ohio Falls near Jeffersonville. While promoting the project, Burr had traveled down the Ohio River on a luxurious flatboat that featured four private rooms, a dining room, two bedrooms and a kitchen complete with a fireplace. But whether he was sincere or not remains, like many events surrounding Burr, a mystery. What is known is that no ground was ever broken for the canal, the enterprise vanished like a puff of smoke and over $120,000 of the stockholders' money disappeared.

To many people, Indiana was an obvious candidate for canals. The state's major river, the Wabash, was a long, rambling 475-mile thoroughfare. It flowed west from the northeast corner of the state at the Ohio border across the northern sections of Indiana and then ambled south near the state's western boundary, connecting there with the Ohio River, which formed Indiana's southern boundary. Despite its many rapids, falls and obstructions, the Wabash's route and its connection with the Ohio River made it a natural water trail for westward-bound travelers willing to brave the dozens of delays and overland portages along the way. The state's other important river, the

---

Indiana's Canal Folly

1832–1846

1832–43 Wabash and Erie Canal
Longer than the Erie Canal and extending through uncharted territory, the Wabash and Erie ran 397 miles from a junction with the Miami and Erie Canal in northwestern Ohio to the Ohio River on the southwest border of Indiana. It was the longest canal in the U.S. Abandoned in 1875.

1832–46 Whitewater Canal
Finally completed to Cincinnati on the Ohio River by a private company, Indiana's second big canal project was begun by the state in 1832 to extend the 74 miles from Hagerstown to the river port.

1837 Economic depression
Bank runs and depression temporarily bring Indiana canal building to a halt.

Whitewater, also stretched to the Ohio, but was much shorter and ambled along the eastern section of the state.

Additionally, as George Washington had pointed out in one of his western surveys, only a short, swampy stretch separated the Wabash from the Maumee River, which stretched eastward across Ohio to Lake Erie. Since many westbound travelers were already using that route, struggling on foot across the marshy land, a canal connection seemed logical there, too.

In fact, any attempt to improve travel and commerce in the state seemed logical to most Indianans. So desperate, in fact, were Indiana citizens that just about everyone seemed to have a different idea about what "internal improvements" the state needed. The call went out for new roads and canals. And some of the more visionary citizens even began to promote the new East Coast fad: a railroad.

For the moment, not many citizens were in favor of a railroad, though. The idea seemed a little far-fetched. And even if the wild promises of the railroad advocates could come true, Indianans, like a lot of midwesterners, didn't much like the idea of having to depend on the rates, schedules and limited access points of privately owned railroad lines.

Most citizens thought that publicly financed canals were the way to go. Given the state's extremely limited funds, however, the problem was how many should be built and where. The clamor centered around the state's two main rivers, the Wabash and the Whitewater. The Wabash supporters wanted a canal that would help bring more settlers and fresh money into the northern and western sections of the state; not unexpectedly, the Whitewater supporters called for a canal that would help the communities along the southeastern sections. As a kind of trial run, with help from federal government land grants, surveyors and engineers were put to work on connecting the Wabash and Maumee rivers near Fort Wayne. The short canal, completed successfully in 1835, immediately renewed the calls from the Wabash and Whitewater factions for action along their favored routes. Lost in the clamor, though, was the fact that the canal commission forced a peaceful Indian tribe, the Potowatomis, from their land at Grand Prairie, along the route of the canal. When the Indians objected and resisted, the army moved in, burned down their villages and rounded up over 800 men, women and children, who were forced to march across the border toward reservations in Kansas. Totally unprepared for the long and difficult journey, nearly one-fifth of the tribe died of starvation and hardship along the way.

This incident, which foreshadowed activities of the railroad barons in the years to come, was not one of Indiana's most honorable moments. But canal mania had come to the state, and even its most sensitive citizens were swept up in the dream.

Like most dreams, Indiana's euphoric visions of canals would soon face harsh reality. But in 1835 few citizens could see anything other than complete success for the state's proposed "internal improvement" systems. Just a few months before the successful completion of the Wabash and Erie's first canal section, a series of complex political agreements and maneuvers resulted in an ambitious plan approved by the state legislature in January 1836. It called for over $13 million worth of canals, turnpikes and even a railroad. The two biggest projects were proposed canals along *both* the Wabash and Whitewater rivers.

Caught up in unquestioning enthusiasm, not only had the state obligated itself to spend much more money than it could afford, but to keep everybody happy it had decided to start all the "internal improvements" at the same time and build them all at once. It was a disastrous decision.

There simply wasn't enough money, trained engineering talent or labor to go around. The usual supply of imported Irish laborers was spread too thin, and competition among the projects for available workers drove wages up sharply. This also drove up the heavy construction costs. At one point, wages were offered at nearly 10 times those usually paid for similar work on other canals, and free roast beef dinner every night was thrown in as an added incentive. "Trained engineers," many of them actually untrained, and not even engineers but friends or relatives of the various members of the board of supervisors, were also awarded contracts and wages far above what would have been usual under normal conditions. The idea was doomed from the start, but there were few impartial observers in Indiana during the 1830s and '40s. Only as the "results" started coming in did some citizens begin to have second thoughts about the whole plan.

Because there was little overall supervision of either the Wabash or Whitewater projects, progress on both was erratic and undisciplined. Often one section of canal would be completed and ready to go into operation, while the connecting sections on either end, supervised and constructed by different crews, were still unfinished. Obviously, full tolls couldn't be collected when only short, unconnected sections of the canals were operational. The public wasn't too happy with the situation. Indianans were beginning to wonder if this was the system that they had once held such hope for.

The first annual financial report, in 1836, didn't make anyone any happier. In the first year, internal improvements, mostly centered around the state's two canals, had cost the state nearly $4 million. At that rate, the cost for the finished system was projected to be over twice the original estimate.

The state was forced to borrow money to continue building its canals. It wasn't a good time to borrow money, however—a serious financial depression was hitting the nation in 1837, with banks curtailing loans and in some cases closing down completely—and there simply wasn't outside money to be had. With work on its internal improvements now virtually at a standstill until payrolls could be met, Indiana turned finally to the federal government. Again, however, its request was turned down.

What was happening to their dream, the citizens of Indiana wanted to know, and how had so much money been lost so quickly?

Investigations were called for and begun, but no one could get an exact accounting of where and how the money had been spent. There had been just too many different hands in the tills and too many systems at work. Had the people been swindled, or were the tremendous expenditures simply due to incompetence? Best guesses maintained that a little bit of both had taken place, but that didn't bring the money back, or do the job that was still left to do.

Making a desperate decision, the state decided to authorize Indiana banks to print up more than $1 million of treasury notes, which could then be borrowed to meet the canal payrolls. That sum was enough to get started again, but the financial hole was growing deeper every day. Finally, after much political and public outcry, the Whitewater Canal was turned over to one private company, which made the final connection with Cincinnati, Ohio in 1846. While other dreamed-of internal improvements were sold to private companies or abandoned completely, it was generally agreed that the important Wabash and Erie Canal, linking the east to the west, had to be finished no matter what the cost.

To finance this decision and meet the canal payrolls, the state began issuing its own money called scrip, with each new batch printed in a different color. Soon the multicolored scrip became the only medium of exchange available along the canal, but its value changed drastically as the work progressed. Scrip was most valuable to townspeople and merchants as canal workers approached their area, but it diminished in value quickly as the workers moved on. Many small businesses went bankrupt as a result, and tempers again flared.

Struggling on, the state managed to finish the Wabash and Erie Canal in 1843, as Ohio completed its adjoining section and made the final link with Indiana. For a while there was jubilation. The long-awaited east-to-west connection had been made. And, as Indiana had hoped, thousands of settlers began pouring in over the new waterway. Any hope for sudden and immediate prosperity, though, had already vanished. Indiana, unable to pay off its loans, was forced to turn the Wabash and Erie over to its creditors.

Still, some of the state's citizens had already begun to make money from the new wave of settlers, and hundreds of new farms and businesses were starting up. In a last burst of hope, the canal was extended farther south to the Ohio River at Evansville, The decision, however, proved to be the final disaster for Indiana's canal system. The last leg of the connection running south from Terre Haute was an echo of all the troubles that had gone before. Debts continued to pile up. More scrip was printed and almost immediately became worthless, bankrupting still more contractors and suppliers. Floods broke through the often poorly constructed sections, and other sections were closed when they failed to meet their operating expenses. Angry farmers, whose taxes had been raised to build the canal, often were stranded between opened and unopened sections, and civil war almost broke out between members of neighboring towns as some along the opened sections prospered while those on the closed ones faced failure.

Almost as soon as it was finished, the new section south of Terre Haute was closed. And within a few years the rest of the canal, which had already begun to deteriorate badly, was quietly shut down.

Had it been worth it? It was obvious to all that Indiana's canal system, the longest yet built in America, was a financial disaster. But it had brought thousands of new settlers into the state and opened up the sparsely populated northern and western sections to slow but steady growth. For many, the ambitious canals had failed. For others, they had succeeded in bringing new hopes and opportunities to the state's inhabitants.

Maybe, as some said, the whole idea had been too ambitious. Maybe, too, as others said, watching the railroads slowly move toward the west, the day of the canal was over, and Indiana had tried not only to do too much, but had done it too late.

CHICAGO REACHES OUT: THE ILLINOIS AND MICHIGAN

Curiously, one of the first canals to be envisioned was one of the last to be built during the canal era. With westbound settlers moving into Indiana, by the mid-1840s Illinois, too, dreamed of becoming a great state. Admitted to the Union in 1818, Illinois had nearly 40% more land available for farming or commerce than Indiana, but less than half its neighbor's population.

The situation was changing, though. The westward migration had begun. In the southern part of the state settlers had begun to arrive from Kentucky, while in the northeastern section the small town of Chicago had begun to see hundreds of settlers arrive by boats on Lake Michigan, some staying and some picking up wagons to head still farther west.

With much of its land still wild or inaccessible except by foot or bone-jarring wagon travel, Illinois's citizens were also calling for "internal improvements" that would keep their state growing.

The I & M Canal connected Lake Michigan with the Illinois River and the Mississippi system. Lewis University Canal Archives

With visions of a bright future glowing in their minds, many Chicago citizens had again started to talk about building a route west that would connect with the Illinois River, then down to the broad, busy Mississippi. Such a Great Lakes–to–Mississippi route would make Chicago the Midwest's major gateway and open up the entire state to continued east-west traffic and prosperity.

The obvious first "improvement," Chicagoans reasoned, was the one proposed many years before by French explorer Louis Joliet—one that would open up a direct link between Chicago and the Illinois River. A canal seemed the obvious choice for many, but others advocated a turnpike or railroad that would connect the town and the river. In fact, the arguments had been raging for years. In 1827 the U.S. Congress had even allotted public land for the Illinois internal improvement program, but despite many studies, reports and suggestions, no one could decide yet if the Chicago–to–Illinois River stretch should be covered by a turnpike or a canal. Once the railroad advocates stepped into the picture later, the stalemate had become even worse.

Finally, in 1834, the state elected Joseph Duncan as governor. Duncan, a forceful and dynamic personality who was used to getting things his own way, was also a strong believer in canals. Under Duncan's sponsorship, a bill was finally pushed through the state legislature that authorized the Illinois and Michigan Canal. Pandemonium broke loose in Chicago.

Illinois and Michigan Canal bank notes of the 1840s. Lewis University Canal Archives

Canal boats moving out onto Lake Michigan from the I & M Canal. Lewis University Canal Archives

Overnight, prices skyrocketed as the small town of a few hundred foresaw itself becoming a great hub of activity. Although the unpaved streets were still incredible cesspools of mud and garbage, construction quickly began on new hotels and restaurants to cater to the expected rush of incoming travelers. And the rush did come. With the town's population swelling to 1,200, the weekly Democrat announced with pride:

> Hardly a vessel arrives that is not crowded with emigrants, and the stage that now runs twice a week from the East is thronged with travelers. The steamship *Pioneer*, which now performs her regular trips to St. Joseph, is also a great accommodation to the travelling community. Loaded teams and covered wagons, laden with families and goods, are daily arriving and settling upon the country back.

By 1837 the town's population grew to 4,000—and construction of the canal could lead only to more growth.

The first ground for the Illinois and Michigan Canal was broken in 1836 on July 4, by then a traditional choice for canal ground breakings and openings. The usual teams of Irish workers were brought in to get the job rolling. By now many of the Irish recruits were "old hands," and they arrived comfortably by boat with their pockets full of money, which, to the citizens' delight, was quickly spent in the bustling streets of Chicago.

Then, after years of waiting, just as suddenly as it had begun, work stopped. The financial depression that began to sweep the nation in late 1836 hit Illinois with a vengeance. The state's financial situation only worsened when, in an attempt to pacify angry citizens located far from the canal route, the state government also agreed to build an expensive and complex system of short railroads. The nationwide crash left little money in the Illinois banks and not much to be found elsewhere.

Even after work on the canal was finally picked up again four years later, the state's commitment to the

Illinois Joins In

1827–1848

1827 U.S. Congress allots public lands for Illinois internal improvement program.

1834 Joseph Duncan, canal advocate, becomes governor of Illinois.

1836 Work begins on the Illinois and Michigan Canal.

1836–37 Depression temporarily halts canal building in Illinois.

1848 The Illinois and Michigan Canal is completed, linking Lake Michigan with the Illinois River and the Mississippi River system.

railroads would keep the canal on the edge of bankruptcy for years.

But the new state administration, believing now that the canal was absolutely necessary for the state's survival, fought to push it to completion. By now, though, in the 1840s, many of the state's citizens outside of the Chicago area had lost their enthusiasm for the canal and the higher taxes it was bringing. Under chief engineer Henry Gooding, who had worked on the Erie, construction crawled ahead toward completion despite a constant financial struggle.

Also crawling ahead were the state's railroads, but few actually ever saw completion. By 1842 most of them were being sold at auction, the half-finished lines long since abandoned. Yet, while Illinois had proved itself unable to build railroads, or at least certainly not at the same time as an expensive canal project, the railroad boom had begun. Sold to a private company, the fledgling Illinois Central Railroad went on to become one of the nation's most important and profitable railroad lines. It also turned out to

be the only profitable railroad venture of the state of Illinois. As part of the sale, in which Illinois also turned over more than 2 million acres to the purchasing company, the state would receive 7% of the railroad's gross earnings.

The Illinois and Michigan Canal was finally completed on April 19, 1848. It ran from Chicago to La Salle on the Illinois River. By then many of the nation's other canals were being dismantled, sold or simply forgotten. The era of the canal, in fact, was coming to a close. Four years later, the first railroad train from the East entered Chicago on the Northern Indiana Railroad. By 1860, 11 different railroad routes fanned out from the city. The Illinois and Michigan Canal would live up to its promise, however; for the next two decades it teamed up with the sprawling railroads to move thousands of passengers and millions of tons of freight from the Great Lakes to the Mississippi—bringing prosperity to the state of Illinois and making a major city of the small town of Chicago.

7

FROM SEA TO SEA: THE PANAMA CANAL 1870–1914

Although the nation's great canal-building boom had long since come to an end, in 1904 American engineers undertook one last great canal. It would be an enormous and costly undertaking, designed to speed transportation from coast to coast in the United States. Besides the difficulty of the project, there was an additional complicating factor. The canal was to be dug on the Isthmus of Panama in Central America. Long and awkward international negotiations preceded even the first turn of a shovel in Panama. By the time the canal was finally finished, the inhospitable climate had caused enormous health problems and hundreds of deaths.

The idea of a canal across the narrow Isthmus of Panama—or some other nearby crossing—between the Atlantic and Pacific oceans had teased explorers, merchants and visionaries for centuries. King Charles V of Spain seriously considered digging a canal in the early 1500s, and so did many others, including the English, the Portuguese, the French and the Americans, all of whom saw the advantage of an interocean canal to provide a shortcut to the West Coast of the Americas and to the Far East beyond. In 1827 the German poet Johann Wolfgang von Goethe, foreseeing the U.S. expansion to the Pacific Coast, told a friend, "It is absolutely indispensable for the United States to effect a passage from the Mexican gulf to the Pacific Ocean; and I am certain they will do it. Would that I might live to see it!"

When discovery of gold in California in 1848 suddenly made crossing to the Pacific Coast a matter of great urgency to thousands of people, the idea of cutting a canal across the Isthmus of Panama became even more attractive to Americans. The 13,000-mile trip around the tip of South America by boat was both costly ($300 for passenger travel) and time consuming (it took six months). The only existing shortcut involved taking a ship to Panama and then making a rugged trip across the narrow tropical isthmus by canoe or mule, followed by another sea voyage north to San Francisco. Such a trip took at least a month, but sporadic shipping schedules on the Pacific side meant that travelers and shipments often languished for weeks waiting to be picked up. Coincidentally, a group of Americans had just obtained a charter to build a railroad across the isthmus from the Colombian government (which had jurisdiction over the area at the time). Although building the railroad took much time and many lives, the Americans were able to help finance their work by charging eager travelers to ride as far as they had track laid and then make their way from there.

In 1879 Ferdinand de Lesseps, a charismatic French engineer who had successfully built the Suez

Panama Canal Facts

1513–1979

1513   Vasco Nuñez de Balboa crosses the isthmus to the Pacific Ocean.

1519   First road across the isthmus.

The Spanish consider building a canal.

1599   The French suggest building a canal.

1799   German scientist Alexander von Humboldt suggests routes.

1855   John Lloyd Stephens puts forth early plans for a canal and the Isthmus of Panama Railroad.

1881–89   The French effort:
The builder of the Suez Canal, Ferdinand de Lesseps, begins work on a canal on the Chagres River. Overcome by mosquitoes, a torrential river and inadequate machinery, he gives up.

1903   The U.S. negotiates to build:
Motivated by the 1849 gold rush to connect East and West more effectively, the U.S. government negotiates with the French, English, Colombian and Panamanian governments for the rights to build a Panama Canal. The Canal Zone is created.

1904   John F. Wallace begins:
Wallace faces disease, chaos and, back in Washington, dissension.

1905   John Stevens replaces Wallace, makes progress, improving living conditions and bringing in more machinery.

President Theodore Roosevelt visits the Panama Canal site.

1907   George Washington Goethals and the Army Corps of Engineers take over.

The Dam.
Building the Gatun Dam to control the Chagres River and create a lake ships could navigate.

The Cut.
Cutting through the continental divide to reduce the number of locks needed (Culebra or Gaillard Cut), engineered by Major David Gaillard, who "moved the mountain" in five years.

The Locks.
Building the canal's six sets of giant double locks.

1914   The first ship sails through:
A small test boat, *Alexandre La Valley*, sails through on January 7, 1914, followed on August 15 by the official opening when the ship *Ancon* sails through the locks. A new era of streamlined water transportation had begun.

1978   New Panama Canal treaties ratified, giving control of the canal to Panama at the end of 1999 and the United States the right to defend the canal's neutrality.

1979   Phasing out U.S. control:
The Canal Zone is returned to Panamanian civil control, with joint U.S.-Panama ownership to the year 1999.

Canal in Egypt, undertook to build a canal in Panama. One hundred thousand French investors believed he was right when he said he could cut a sea-level channel through the isthmus—requiring no locks. But the proposed canal differed from the Suez in a number of ways. Though shorter, the Panama Canal needed to surmount heights of 330 feet—far more than the mere 50-foot rise of the Suez. The ground was rock, not sand. And, in contrast to Egypt's dry, desert heat, Panama's oppressive tropical heat and drenching rains sabotaged both men and machines, and bred insects that caused deadly bouts of malaria and yellow fever. De Lesseps began digging in 1881. Six years later, in 1887, he finally admitted that locks would be necessary, after all. In 1888 his company announced bankruptcy, de Lesseps was shown to have mismanaged the project, allowing rampant graft and siphoning of funds, and he was convicted, denounced and ruined.

Meanwhile, the United States had not given up on a Central American canal crossing, but negotiations with Colombia to buy rights to the canal begun by the French in Panama were not smooth. In a move that still haunts U.S.-Latin American relations, under President Theodore Roosevelt the United States backed a Panamanian nationalist movement in revolt against Colombia and immediately recognized the new Republic of Panama. By November 1903 Roosevelt's secretary of state, John Hay, had signed a treaty with Panama. In exchange for a $10 million cash down payment and $250,000 a year, the United States would receive, in perpetuity, a zone five miles wide on either side of the canal for its 50-mile length. What Colombia and its allies viewed as Americans' high-handed interference and obvious self-interest left deep fissures between the United States and nearly all of its Latin American neighbors. The move also fired up Roosevelt's critics at home.

But to all of them, Teddy Roosevelt had this message: "Tell them that I am going to make the dirt fly on the Isthmus." And fly it did.

To the French, the United States paid $4 million for the canal as far as they had dug it and for their construction machinery. When the Americans arrived, they found literally millions of dollars' worth of rusted equipment and old railroad locos and cars cluttering up the right of way.

But the French had also left the beginnings of a canal—25 feet deep and 75 feet wide, running 11 miles inland from Colón to Bohio. The Americans were also able to repair many of the French machines and get three machine shops back up and working. The Americans restored and put to use more than 1,000 of the over 2,000 buildings the French had left.

WALLACE'S WOBBLY START

John Findley Wallace, the first chief resident engineer, arrived in Panama with his wife and two coffins, one for each of them, or at least so the story went. Haunted by the rampancy of disease in Panama, a place he once called a "God-forsaken country," he had morbid premonitions about his fate. His engineering credentials were strong, but for this job his enthusiasm never seemed to rise to the occasion. He neglected to solve the pressing problems of housing workers, and he never came to terms with the malaria and yellow fever that soon raged among his work crews. He failed to give the canal's medical officer, William Crawford Gorgas, the support he needed to fight the insidious diseases. And he failed to provide leadership for the crews. Many of the Americans who signed up early on were drifters, railroad men who could no longer get hired in the States or inexperienced men who got their jobs through political pull. They were not easily led, but Wallace was also no leader.

Nonetheless, work began immediately—even though no decision had yet been made about exactly what kind of canal they were building. Would it be a sea-level, lock-free canal, as de Lesseps had originally attempted? Or a canal with locks climbing over the mountain range that ran through Panama? The issue remained undecided.

Initially, a seven-man commission located 2,000 miles away directed the work. Communications between these and the engineers on-site were poor at best, and the commission's penny-pinching approach (designed to avoid the financial disaster de Lesseps had faced) made a difficult job nearly impossible. The red tape was endless. Six separate vouchers had to be signed in Panama just to use a hand cart, and carpenters were required to get a signed authorization to saw anything over 10 feet in length.

At the height of all the troubles, even a case of bubonic plague developed. Although the plague never caused serious trouble, deaths from malaria and yellow fever were adding up each day. Wallace left Panama with his wife, turning in his resignation in June 1905—and both angering and disappointing those who had appointed him. Many felt that he was irresponsible, abandoning his post at the worst time

William Gorgas:
Fighting Malaria and Yellow Fever in Panama

Disease wasn't a new enemy of canal builders when Americans began work on the Isthmus of Panama; it was just more rampant. When William Gorgas arrived as chief sanitary officer in 1904 with his wife, Maria, he faced conditions that one reporter described as "hideous," with no plumbing or sewers and many people living in shacks on stilts stuck in a "vast expanse of black water covered with green scum." The causes of yellow fever and malaria—and recognition of the role mosquitoes played in their spread—had only recently been discovered. But William Gorgas, an army physician, was an expert. He had fought against yellow fever, especially, in both Texas and Havana, Cuba. By destroying the places mosquitoes bred, he had cut the cases of yellow fever in one year from 1,400 to 37 and, finally, to none. He had studied the medical records of the French effort in Panama, visited the Suez Canal and attended a world conference on tropical medicine in Cairo.

And yet the Canal Commission ignored his requests for adequate help and supplies necessary for the fight. They sent seven people and virtually no supplies at all. No wire screens for the windows. Not even any disinfectant. Few members of Congress even believed that the mosquito carried disease. And he got no cooperation for his planned war against mosquitoes from Chief Engineer Wallace, either, who was distrustful of Gorgas's ideas about mosquitoes, malaria and yellow fever and regarded his work as purely experimental.

Meanwhile, the mosquitoes, of course, were breeding everywhere in the warm, moist tropical climate, wherever a pool of calm water lay—in a cow's footprint, a bowl of water, a stagnant pond, a cistern, a rain barrel. With no running water in Colón, drinking water was typically kept indoors in earthenware jars. The mosquitoes bred there too. And in the hospitals, to keep ants away from the patients, each bed leg was set in a plate of water—providing one more convenient breeding ground. At the excavation, marshes and the canal line would provide still more. With one female mosquito laying up to 120 eggs that mature in less than 10 days, the problem multiplied astronomically. As soon as more workers were brought in, Gorgas knew, the mosquito population would thrive even more.

Yellow fever started to hit hard in November 1904, resulting in many deaths, and reports of the deplorable conditions began to filter back to the States. In what later became known as "The Great Scare," two-thirds of all Americans left Panama for home.

and leaving out of fear. His reputation never really recovered.

JOHN STEVENS DIGS IN

John Wallace was replaced by railroader John F. Stevens, recommended to Roosevelt by Great Northern Railroad magnate James J. Hill, who said he considered Stevens the "best construction engineer in the country." Stevens was 52 years old, heavyset, experienced and weathered—every bit the tough engineer. An outdoorsman, Stevens had spent most of his life learning to survive—and had experienced many adventures, including Indian and wolf attacks, in the American Northwest. He had little formal training but had learned surveying and had worked on various

railroads before (and after) joining James Hill on the construction of the Great Northern. Hill, a rugged individualist himself, had great respect for Stevens, of whom he once said, "He is always in the right place at the right time and does the right thing without asking about it."

By the time Stevens arrived at Colón in Panama in July 1905, almost an entire year had been lost under Wallace as chief engineer. Stevens, a quiet, determined engineer, is said to have told the men shortly after his arrival, "There are three diseases in Panama. They are yellow fever, malaria, and cold feet; and the greatest of these is cold feet."

Stevens was a question asker. He probed and probed to find the information and men he needed. Known as "Big Smoke," because of his ever-puffing

Spraying larvacide to prevent mosquito breeding near Miraflores in the Canal Zone, 1910. Library of Congress

Gorgas continued studying the life cycle and habits of the mosquito to improve his tactics and, finally, funds came through. A thousand workers sprayed streams and swamp water with oil, cleared brush and cut grass, drained swamps and destroyed garbage. According to an account written by Maria Gorgas, at one point Goethals, who was by that time in charge of the Canal Zone, told Gorgas that each mosquito he killed cost the government $10. To which Gorgas replied, "But just think, one of those 10-dollar mosquitoes might bite you, and what a loss that would be to the country."

By 1905 Gorgas and his "medical army" had won the war against yellow fever, with many sanitary conditions vastly improved. But the battle against malaria was a harder one. The species of mosquito that spread malaria bred in more farflung areas than the yellow fever bearer, which liked to be near humans—and completely eliminating them from the jungles and swamps of the isthmus proved a nearly impossible, ongoing task.

cigar, he was also generally respected as a man who could get things done.

Unlike Wallace, Stevens liked Dr. Gorgas from the start. As soon as he was officially in charge he ordered that the medical officer should have all the men and cooperation he needed in his medical work. Soon Gorgas was leading a health campaign the intensity and cost of which the world had never seen.

Stevens brought many organizational techniques that had worked for him when he'd worked with Jim Hill. One approach was to find the "best men" for particular jobs and give them tremendous authority in getting those jobs done. "You won't get fired if you do something," he would tell his key men. "You will if you don't do anything. Do something if it is wrong, for you can correct that, but there is no way to correct nothing."

Stevens saw much of the canal building as a "railroad" problem, and he brought in fresh railroad men to help solve it. Stevens found the Panama Railroad too light—almost a toy. Within the year he built a new one, double tracked with heavy rails and capable of carrying the heaviest and biggest locomotives and cars—as had been done on the Great Northern. He also brought in a professional army of yardmen, switchmen, dispatchers, mechanics and engineers to run the railroad. Stevens knew that the railroad was the lifeline for everything—food, supplies, labor, equipment—and he created a strong one.

He tripled the work force within the first few months, and by the end of 1906 over 24,000 men were working on the canal project. The work force was larger than the total number of workers on the Union

Digging at Culebra Cut in December 1904, during the time John Wallace was in charge. Library of Congress

Pacific during the race to finish the first American transcontinental railroad and larger than the French had ever had in Panama.

Stevens also worked to improve morale by building baseball fields, improving food, encouraging married men to bring their wives and families, and setting up better living quarters and conditions.

From an engineering standpoint, Stevens saw the actual building of the canal as simpler than some engineering projects of the time that were less in the public eye. There were no major new techniques needed, no problems with supplies, money or purchasing rights-of-way, no traffic to worry about—only the canal's huge scale made it challenging. "There is no element of mystery involved in it," he said. "The problem is one of magnitude and not miracles."

Stevens focused on what he knew—the challenges of moving large amounts of excavated tonnage in the fastest and most efficient way possible. For this he needed no miracles. But about canals he knew nothing. And he didn't know he would not be building a "sea-level canal."

Even after arriving he had not been told, because no one had decided yet what kind of a canal he was to build. Later he said it was a little like being told to build a house without knowing whether the finished project was to be a tollhouse or a capitol building.

Teddy Roosevelt had set up a board composed of eight Americans and five Europeans to study the problem of what kind of a canal to build. Meanwhile Stevens was doing what was necessary to get his railroad and supporting systems up and operating. And he began to see the advantages that locks could provide. As proposed by its backers, the sea-level canal would be narrow and torturously twisting, subject to landslides and blockage.

Roosevelt liked John Stevens. He liked knowing Stevens was a "reader" who reread favorite books, such as Mark Twain's *Huckleberry Finn*, over and over again as Roosevelt did.

Stevens, though, was not used to dealing with politicians or Congress. He thought that he was going to be able to work as he had with James Hill on the Great Northern Railroad. He wanted to build the project by contracts, picking different companies and men for the different jobs—but he was unprepared for Congress's red tape and its decree that contracts should be given only after open bids.

Less than two years after taking the job, Stevens also suddenly resigned. No one knew why, though stories flew about discontent with political maneuverings in Washington and interference from Roosevelt. Stevens, perhaps not literally intending to resign, wrote to the President:

To me the canal is only a big ditch, and its great utility when completed, has never been so apparent to me, as it seems to be to others. . . . There has never been a day since my connection with this enterprise that I could not have gone back to the United States and occupied positions that to me, were far more satisfactory. Some of them, I would prefer to hold, if you will pardon my candor, than the Presidency of the United States.

Whatever the exact turn of events, Roosevelt accepted the resignation and Big Smoke's days on the Panama Canal came to an end.

GOETHALS GETS IT DONE

Exasperated, Roosevelt decided to place the canal construction "in charge of men who will stay on the job until I get tired of having them there." In effect, he assigned the project to the U.S. Army Corps of Engineers—although all the army men he now placed in charge were officially on detached duty. The President could be sure that those in top positions, who were mostly West Pointers, would not quit. Not only would quitting be unthinkable, but it would also end their military careers. The canal's third chief engineer, Major George W. Goethals, took charge in April 1907.

Tall, with gray hair and a bronzed face, Goethals was a career officer in the army, a former West Point instructor in civil and military engineering. He already had construction of one canal to his credit, at Muscle Shoals on the Tennessee River. This 49-year-old, Brooklyn-born man of Dutch descent saw his role in Panama as the head of an "expeditionary force to tame nature." And from the moment he arrived, he was in full command.

Although Goethals maintained that his regime would be no more military than his popular predecessor's, he was no-nonsense, dedicated and demanding. Typical were his remarks to one of his foremen while inspecting a work crew's progress.

"You are not very far along," Goethals remarked bluntly.

"I know, Colonel," came the reply. "But we are doing our best."

"I don't expect you to do your best," Goethals barked. "I expect you to complete your work on time."

Goethals brought stern order and discipline to the canal—but he also cleverly increased progress by encouraging rivalry among the various work crews. He established a newspaper, the *Canal Record*, that published weekly statistics on each crew's progress and costs to stoke the fires, and constantly called for new record accomplishments.

Moreover, Roosevelt once again reorganized the Canal Commission. This time Goethals was appointed head of the commission as well as chief engineer. This gave him total and complete authority.

Most of the canal route had already been decided under Stevens. From the breakwaters of the Caribbean the canal would head south at sea level a short distance. (Overall, the canal actually runs northwest-southeast through the narrow strip of land that loops west to east around the Bay and Gulf of Panama to connect Costa Rica with Colombia.) Then an 85-foot ascent would lift boats via three locks to a man-made lake 23 miles long. At the far end of the lake, the nine-mile Culebra Cut would bisect the hills of Panama's rocky Continental Divide. At San Miguel, on the Pacific side of the cut, a small artificial lake (Miraflores Lake) would separate another lock from the last two locks leading down to the Pacific.

In fact, the plan generally followed the one proposed about two dozen years earlier by Godin de Lépinay at an international meeting of the Geographical Society in Paris in 1879. "Dam the Chagres and the Rio Grande [rivers] near the sea," he had said. "Raise the water level to eighty feet above sea level, construct locks, and then your cuttings in the Obispo Valley and across Culebra will be eighty feet less deep, thus enormously reducing your work." The job now for Goethals was to get it dug. He did, however, make some key changes: to widen Culebra Cut through the hills to 300 feet at the bottom, four times the width planned for the French canal; to widen the locks to 110 feet so the navy's largest battleships could pass through; to build a breakwater on the Pacific side to prevent deposits of silt, or loose particles of sand and sediment, from being washed up by the strong currents there; and to change the location of the Pacific locks from Sosa Hill to Miraflores. All his changes enhanced the military usefulness of the Canal—with a channel and locks big enough to accommodate the big battleships then on the drawing boards and with the Pacific locks pulled back from the shore far enough to be safe from bombardment and sabotage from unfriendly ships. Of course, bombardment from the air did not yet occur to anyone as a possibility.

The Culebra Cut (later known as Gaillard Cut, after Major du Bose Gaillard, who oversaw most of the digging) was the most demanding part of the whole project, an undertaking whose proportions boggled the mind. Writing at the time, Joseph Bucklin Bishop described "the grim, forbidding, perpendicular walls of rock" separated by "the steadily widening and deepening chasm between" as filled with an army of men and machines. A staggering total of 96 million cubic yards of rocks and dirt had to be dug out and removed to provide a channel for the canal. The job employed 6,000 workers drilling, blasting, hauling rock and earth, and operating the railroad and the steam shovels. About 500 trainloads were hauled each day to dump sites. In March 1910 one huge steam shovel set the record for one machine by excavating 70,000 cubic yards in 26 days.

The machinery—although nothing like modern equipment—was like none ever before used. Huge, 95-ton steam shovels (three times the size of those used by the French) lifted eight tons of material per scoop as they lumbered forward mounted on railroad carriages that moved along tracks laid down in front

of them. Amazingly, all the work was done by only 50 to 60 machines working at any one time along the nine-mile man-made canyon, and everything was moved by rail—no trucks at all were used. In 1907 alone the great steam shovels excavated as much as 1 million cubic yards in a month (a volume of dirt the size of the Empire State Building). Under Goethals 2 million and then 3 million cubic yards soon became commonplace. The great canyon buzzed with the movement of 140 locomotives and 3,700 flatcars moving earth and rock over 130 miles of track. Workers blasted 60 million tons of dynamite—placed in holes totaling a depth, if strung end to end, of over 65 miles. Described by one steam shovel operator as "Hell's Gorge," the channel practically boiled with noise and activity by day, with work crews coming in by rail at night to repair the battered equipment for the next day. Despite all the apparent confusion, though, the entire operation was perfectly coordinated, shovels, workers, dynamite, and trains moving like clockwork in a tightly scheduled plan laid out in advance each

Culebra Cut, looking south toward the Pacific, in August 1907. Library of Congress

day. When Culebra Cut was finally completed in 1913, after seven years of intensive labor, its total cost came to $10 million a mile.

The human cost was equally high. Hundreds of men were killed or maimed, blown to bits by dynamite, crushed under railroad wheels, struck by flying rock. In one day alone in December 1908, 23 men were killed in a dynamite blast. In his epic book *The Path Between the Seas*, David McCullough quotes one black laborer recalling "Man die, get blow up, get kill or get drown, during the time someone asked where is Brown? He died last night and bury. Where is Jerry? He dead a little before dinner and buried. So on and so on all the time."

Great slides of mud and earth also created one of the greatest obstacles along the Culebra Cut—one that early advisors to Roosevelt vastly underestimated, despite difficulties the French had faced with the same problem.

William H. Burr, of Roosevelt's international advisory board, had proclaimed confidently, "All that is necessary to remedy such a condition is simply to excavate the clay or to drain it to keep the water out. It is not a new problem. It is no formidable feature of the work."

He was wrong. Landslides continued to present a constant danger. While some historians claim that few lives and little machinery were lost beneath the giant, slow-moving mud slippages, the great slides halted the work again and again, often lasting days or even weeks, and leaving huge, sloping hills "covering many acres," according to Bishop, "and reaching far back into the hills." One slide, lasting days, dumped nearly 500,000 cubic yards of mud into the canal, and often miles of muddy earth were on the move, slowly yet inevitably reburying everything in the way. Some slides were so dramatic, though, that they would literally wipe out entire months of work in a few hours. Large, small and medium slides happened almost all the time at some place or other inside the cut.

Meanwhile, to create the 23-mile Gatun Lake, the artificial lake on the Atlantic end of the canal, workers built an earth dam using 30 million tons of mud, clay and rock. Back in the United States, doubts abounded on the issue of whether the Gatun Dam would hold. Only a few years earlier, in 1889, a similar earthen dam at Johnstown, Pennsylvania had collapsed, killing 2,000 people when millions of tons of water rushed into the Conemaugh Valley. Newspapers reported that rock heaps at the Gatun dam site had settled into

soft ground beneath, and skeptics made dire predictions. But this time the engineers knew what they were doing. When finished in 1913, the huge mile-and-a-half-long dam measured 105 feet high and a half-mile thick at the base. The lake that formed behind it covered 164 square miles of land—the largest man-made body of water in the world at the time.

At the eastern end of the dam, built up from a concrete floor, the Gatun Locks emerged. Designed mostly by Lieutenant Colonel Harry Foote Hodges, the mammoth locks took four years in all to build, beginning with those at Gatun in August 1909. They were massive, 1,000 feet long, 110 feet wide, set side by side in pairs so that traffic could travel both ways at once. If one of the locks were stood on end, it would be higher than the Eiffel Tower. Between the locks ran a wall 60 feet thick, with a 13-foot concrete floor beneath. Seven-foot-thick steel lock gates were at least 47 feet high and weighed 390 tons; others were nearly 90 feet high and over 700 tons. The locks at Miraflores, at the opposite end of the canal, are the highest in the system at 82 feet—about the height of a six-story building. Such a height is necessary because the tides of the Pacific vary so greatly.

These gigantic structures not only stood, they were huge mechanical devices made of thousands of moving parts and controlled by some 1,500 electrical motors. Huge forms were built for the walls, and workers poured bucket after bucket of concrete from above to fill the great frames. Within the walls, forms within the forms created a catacomb of tunnels and passageways. Each great concrete basin, when finished, was like a a giant tub, both ends closed by the huge steel gates. The impression was of looking down a broad, level street nearly five blocks long with a solid wall of six-story buildings on either side.

Called "the greatest engineering feat of the ages," the Panama Canal was unquestionably a great wonder of human achievement. Yet, ironically, when the first boat, the SS *Ancon*, locked through on August 15, 1914, only a handful of people even took notice. There was no fanfare to greet the *Ancon* as it locked down to the Pacific Ocean at Miraflores. No champagne bottles or fireworks. Several thousand miles away, World War I had just begun, and the world was looking the other way.

At first, because of the war, not much traffic moved through the canal—only about four or five ships a day, or about 2,000 a year until 1918. In 1915 about 15 million tons passed through, and $4 million in tolls was collected. But by 10 years later the canal was as important to shipping as the Suez, with 5,000 ships locking through annually. Some 14,000 a year locked through in the years following World War II. When channel lighting was added in 1966, night crossings began, and ships began passing through at a rate of more than one an hour, every hour of the day, every day of the year. The annual tolls collected peaked in 1970 at $100 million even though rates had not changed since the canal was opened.

THE PANAMA CANAL TODAY

By the 1960s, though, the key importance of the Panama Canal had begun to taper off for the United States. With its locks not large enough for the U.S. Navy's big aircraft carriers, the canal had lost its strategic significance for the military. Some military experts even suggested that the presence of U.S. troops

in Panama threatened the canal by making it a target of aggression. And the canal always remains vulnerable to sabotage by Panamanian nationalists upset by U.S. presence there.

As a commercial transportation artery, the canal lost much of its dominance in international trade during the OPEC oil embargo in the 1970s. At that time some 20 to 30 ships a day passed through the canal—about 5 percent of world trade by volume, with tolls averaging about $10,000 per ship. Traveling through the 50-mile waterway in one hour, 24 hours a day, ships could still save some $50,000 in time and mileage. As Donald G. Schmidt, a deputy director of the Panama Canal Commission, explained in 1988, "Canal traffic grew steadily every year from World War II until 1973." But at that time, he pointed out, "We got hit with the oil shock and we suffered the same as everyone else did." Until then, oil-carrying ships had been the canal's major source of revenue. Discovery of oil on the North Slope in Alaska in 1977 bolstered

The upper locks at Gatun, with a view of the west chamber, looking north. This photo, taken June 7, 1912, shows the upper guard gates, the operating gates, the intermediate gates and the safety gates in process of construction. Library of Congress

The east and west chambers of Miraflores Locks, November 1912. Library of Congress

traffic on the canal for a time, but completion of the Alaska pipeline in 1977 and another in Panama in 1982 drew away almost all of the canal's oil traffic, and canal traffic decreased greatly. Experts estimated that traffic on the canal would increase annually only about 2 to 2½ percent in the last decade before 1999.

At that time, under the terms of a treaty forged in 1977 between Panama's president Omar Torrijos and U.S. president Jimmy Carter (the Torrijos-Carter treaty), the Canal Zone and the canal would be turned over to Panama.

Historical Headlines

1870–1914

1871   The first Ohio River railroad crossing is built, an iron-and-wood truss between Bellaire, Ohio and Benwood, West Virginia.

1874   St. Louis Bridge (later renamed the Eads Bridge) is completed, the first to cross the Mississippi. A railroad bridge, it is the first major steel construction in the United States.

1876   Collapsing railroad bridges begin to become a serious problem: 80 people die and 35 more are injured in railroad bridge collapse at Ashtabula Creek in Ohio.

1878   Philadelphia installs electric arc lights.

1880   U.S. population has swelled to 50.1 million.

1883   The Brooklyn Bridge, largest suspension bridge in the world up to this time, is completed.

1888   After 17 years of discussion and construction, the Poughkeepsie Bridge (a railroad bridge) is completed across the Hudson River in upstate New York.

1889   Expansion continues: Oklahoma Territory (previously Indian Territory) is opened to white settlers.

1892   In Chicago, the first electric automobile (made by William Morrison of Des Moines, Iowa) is driven.

        Frank and Charles Duryea of Massachusetts make the first American gasoline automobile.

1894   German inventor Rudolf Diesel invents the Diesel engine.

1898   Spanish-American War begins; the Treaty of Paris is signed in December with the United States emerging as a recognized world power.

        William McKinley takes a ride in a Stanley Steamer, becoming the first President to ride in an automobile.

1903   A Packard car travels from San Francisco to New York in 52 days in the first trip across the United States by automobile.

        Henry Ford establishes the Ford Motor Company.

        December 17. Orville and Wilbur Wright make the first successful manned flight of a motorized aircraft at Kitty Hawk, North Carolina.

        The Williamsburg Bridge, over the East River in New York City, becomes the first large suspension bridge to be constructed using steel towers.

1909   The 16th Amendment to the Constitution, granting Congress the power to levy and collect income tax, is sent to the states for ratification.

1912   New Mexico becomes the 47th and Arizona the 48th state. No new states will be admitted until Alaska and Hawaii are admitted to the Union in 1958 and 1959 respectively.

1914   World War I breaks out in Europe.

        The United States completes the Panama Canal, originally started by the French 33 years before.

8

CANALS CONTINUE: INLAND WATERWAYS IN THE 20TH CENTURY

With completion of the Panama Canal, America's love affair with canal construction finally drew to a close. While the Panama Canal continued to be a vital east-west navigation link well into the late 20th century, on the continent the canal network had long since ceased to be as important to the country's transportation system as it once had been. First railroads in the late 1800s, then highways and airways in the 20th century took over as primary transportation networks for both cargo and passengers. But the Panama Canal was by no means the last important artificial waterway Americans built for transportation. And, especially in bulk transport—conveying materials such as grain and coal—canal traffic continues to play an important role in the country's overall transportation system. Today over 25,000 miles of canals in the United States are in use, serving 38 states and carrying 2 billion tons of freight each year.

The barges that travel today's canals vary in type. Open hopper barges carry coal, ores and minerals. Covered hopper barges provide protection for grain or some types of chemicals. Modern hopper barges can carry an enormous amount of cargo—up to 1,500 tons, or about as much as 14 jumbo rail cars or 50 large trucks. Tank barges transport liquid cargo such as petroleum, while deck barges can carry sand, gravel or heavy equipment on their broad, flat decks.

In addition to their commercial uses, many canals, both old and new, continue to serve as resort areas and historic preservations of a bygone era, serving thousands of excursions, hundreds of thousands of pleasure craft and millions of interested visitors annually. In November 1986 the canals of New York State completed one of the busiest seasons of the century, with more than 123,000 pleasure boats locking through them. In addition, commercial tug operations consistently reach 400,000 tons annually on New York canals, where they provide an important artery for barge transport of gasoline, kerosene, jet fuel, asphalt, cement, machinery and molasses.

Of the many modern canal and waterway projects, two serve as excellent examples of both frustrations and triumphs in building major waterway connections today: the St. Lawrence Seaway between the Great Lakes and the Atlantic, and the Tennessee-Tombigbee connecting the waterways of the southeast United States with the Gulf of Mexico.

THE ST. LAWRENCE SEAWAY

A joint Canadian-U.S. venture on the upper St. Lawrence River, the St. Lawrence Seaway is part of a great inland waterway stretching 2,342 miles from the Atlantic Ocean to Duluth, Minnesota on Lake Supe-

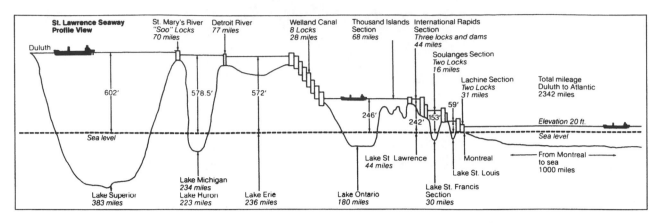

St. Lawrence Seaway Profile View. Duluth — 602' — Sea level — Lake Superior 383 miles. St. Mary's River "Soo" Locks 70 miles — 578.5' — Lake Michigan 234 miles, Lake Huron 223 miles. Detroit River 77 miles — 572' — Lake Erie 236 miles. Welland Canal 8 Locks 28 miles. Thousand Islands Section 68 miles — 246' — Lake Ontario 180 miles. International Rapids Section Three locks and dams 44 miles — 242' — Lake St. Lawrence 44 miles. Soulanges Section Two Locks 16 miles — 153' — Lake St. Francis Section 30 miles. Lachine Section Two Locks 31 miles — 59' — Montreal, Lake St. Louis. Total mileage Duluth to Atlantic 2342 miles — Elevation 20 ft. Sea level. From Montreal to sea 1000 miles.

The St. Lawrence Seaway, serving both the United States and Canada, opened up ship passage from the Great Lakes to the Atlantic Ocean along the St. Lawrence River. St. Lawrence Seaway Development Corporation

A lake vessel heading upbound at the Eisenhower Lock on the St. Lawrence Seaway. St. Lawrence Seaway Development Corporation

rior—enabling oceangoing vessels to travel and put into port on the Great Lakes. Its history goes back to the Sault Ste. Marie (or "Soo") Canal, built in 1797 by Canadians to join Lake Superior and Lake Huron. Other Canadian canals along the route followed—the Lachine Canal in 1821–1825 to circumvent the rapids above Montreal in Quebec, the Welland Canal in Canada (1824–1829) to connect Lakes Erie and Ontario, bypassing Niagara Falls. By 1887 three more canals had been constructed, and the whole system had been deepened to 14 feet.

Discovery of copper and iron ore deposits in the Lake Superior region also awakened American interest in the route from the lakes to the sea, and in 1855 the United States rebuilt the "Soo" Canal (to replace the Canadian canal destroyed in the War of 1812). But formation of the Deep Waterways Commission, authorized by the U.S. Congress in 1895, signaled the beginning of real involvement, in cooperation with Canada, and surveying began. No construction followed, however, although the Canadians once again refurbished the Welland Canal in 1932. Franklin D. Roosevelt authorized another study in 1940, but still nothing happened. Annoyed, Canadian Prime Minister Lester Pearson remarked in 1951, "The biggest and longest dragging of feet I have known in my entire life is that of the Americans on the St. Lawrence." Work did not finally begin until Congress approved a construction start in May 1954.

Two of the Seaway's seven locks are on the American side—the Eisenhower and the Snell locks, with the greatest lift, of 45 feet, at Snell Lock. Once begun, the work moved quickly, with the Seaway opened to traffic on April 25, 1959, enabling oceangoing vessels to dock at ports such as Duluth, Detroit, Chicago, Cleveland, Buffalo and Erie.

THE TENNESSEE-TOMBIGBEE WATERWAY

Completed in 1985, the Tennessee-Tombigbee is a 234-mile waterway, the largest ever undertaken by the U.S. Army Corps of Engineers. Linking two major rivers in Alabama and Mississippi, it established a waterway link to the Gulf of Mexico from America's heartland, with connections to 16,000 miles of inland waterways. Though not as deep as the Panama Canal (with a 9-foot-deep barge channel compared with the Panama's 45-foot ship channel), the Tenn-Tom Waterway required removal of one-third more earth—an enormous 307 million cubic yards. The Tenn-Tom also rises 341 feet, a lift more than three and a half times greater than the Panama's. To build it, the Corps used 33,000 tons of steel and enough concrete to construct a 120-story building covering an entire football field. It took more than 12 years to build, with 3,000 people working for 25 million man-hours.

The most difficult section was a 39-mile cut at Bay Springs, through the geographical divide (known as

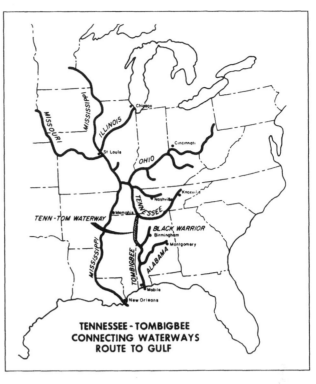

By connecting the Tennessee River with the Tombigbee River in Alabama, the Tennessee-Tombigbee Waterway linked America's heartland with the Gulf of Mexico. U.S. Army Corps of Engineers

A Canadian laker, the Quebeçois, *headed east, or downbound, on the St. Lawrence Seaway. While this vessel is not an ocean-going ship, the Seaway accommodates many ocean vessels as well. St. Lawrence Seaway Development Corporation*

U.S. Canals in the 20th-Century—Facts

1903–19   New York State Barge Canal
Incorporates 363 miles of the old Erie Canal.

1905   Gulf Intracoastal Waterway
Like the Atlantic Intracoastal, a federal project linking artificial and natural waterways between ports along the Gulf of Mexico from Texas to Florida. First conceived in 1905 to link inland ports with ocean-going traffic.

1914   Cape Code Canal
Cuts across the neck of the Cape in Massachusetts.

1919   Chesapeake-Delaware Canal
Originally built in 1829, with new construction in 1919. Connects Delaware and Chesapeake bays.

1927   Atlantic Intracoastal Waterway
A complex series of artificial channels linking natural waterways between the ports along the Atlantic coast from Boston to Key West. A federal project authorized in part by legislation passed in 1927, like the Gulf Intracoastal Waterway, it makes extensive use of established canals along the coast.

1933   Illinois Waterway
Artificial and natural channels linking the Mississippi River to Lake Michigan via the Illinois River.

1957   The St. Lawrence Seaway
Utilizes several canals and sets of locks to link the Great Lakes to the North Atlantic Ocean, making Chicago a seaport. Includes the use of paired locks (Welland Canal) so that ships can travel up and down the waterway at the same time.

1963   Sacramento Deep-Water Ship Canal
Links Sacramento, California with San Francisco Bay, making Sacramento a seaport.

1985   Tennessee-Tombigbee Waterway
Begun in 1979, completed in 1985, 234 miles long, connecting about 16,000 miles of inland waterways to create a shortcut from Midwestern and Southeastern areas to the Gulf of Mexico.

Barge traffic moves through the canal below Lock D on the Tenn-Tom Waterway. U.S. Army Corps of Engineers

The "Divide Cut" through the high ridge at Bay Springs was the most difficult section of the Tenn-Tom Waterway to construct. U.S. Army Corps of Engineers

the "Divide Cut") between the two river valleys. One-half of all the material removed to create the waterway was dug from this high ridge, where 1,400 men worked in two 10-hour shifts a day until the job was finished.

The 10 locks along the canal are 110 feet wide and 600 feet long so that a towboat and eight standard barges can lock through all at once. The average "stair-step" level they raise or lower is 28 feet—although the one at Bay Springs is a giant 84 feet. As a towboat-barge combination locks through, in about 20 or 30 minutes, some 14 million gallons of water move in or out of the chamber—40 million at the huge Bay Springs lock.

The Tenn-Tom's first shipment headed out from New Orleans, Louisiana to Sheffield, Alabama on the Tennessee River, carrying more than 2½ million gallons of oil aboard a four-barge tow. Its towboat, the *Eddie Waxler*, entered the Tennessee-Tombigbee Waterway on January 14, 1985, pushing its four barges ahead of it. The whole trip was a distance of only 620 miles, just over half what the shipment would have traveled using the Mississippi River system instead.

Today, major shipments of coal, petroleum products, metallic ores and chemicals travel the Tenn-Tom

Constructing a lock and dam on the Tennessee-Tombigbee Waterway. U.S. Army Corps of Engineers

The dredge Tenn-Tom *begins the final cut through the 120-foot-thick railroad embankment near Amory, Mississippi. This was the last obstacle to a through waterway connecting the Tennessee and Tombigbee rivers.* U.S. Army Corps of Engineers

24 hours a day. Once open, the Tenn-Tom has not only provided a major commercial artery but also a recreational area for thousands of boaters. Even today, though, a voyage along a canal remains an adventure nearly as unpredictable as a trip on the James River and Kenawha in the mid-19th century, as canal enthusiast Addison Austin shows in this account of his 1985 test of the new Tenn-Tom waters in his craft the *Yankee Doodle:*

The upriver trip to the first lock at Coffeeville was much slower than expected, with quite strong river currents, morning fogs, an engine coolant hose failure, and a side trip to explore the remains of old lock

one. The lockmaster at Coffeeville said that Bobby's Fish Camp, just upriver, had groceries, ice and a restaurant. The hoped for slack water above the lock was not to be, with currents as strong as below, making the stop at Bobby's a bit tricky. After finally getting lashed to a branch and a protruding tree root, it turned out the fish camp's restaurant only opened weekends, there would be no ice until morning, and the only food available was five-pound and larger bags of frozen local catfish. Another boat limped in with a bent propeller from debris in the river. . . .

As Austin's account readily shows, canals have changed, and yet, in a way, they haven't.

From the first canal built in the United States to the most recent, "big ditches" have helped to implement a dream for Americans—a dream of a better life, of a more direct route to save both time and money, of a better way of getting from here to there. Today waterways form an important part of an "intermodal" transportation system that combines different modes of transportation—canals, railways, trucks, airlines and transocean shipping—to connect the United States with the international marketplace. For modern-day "canawlers" plying the inland water routes, canals still provide an adventure. And the wild and woolly days when "canal fever" charged the nations' visions will always remain an important part of American lore and history.

Historical Headlines

1915–1990

1917   April 2. The United States declares war on Germany.

1918   President Wilson presents his 14 Points that he feels are necessary to peace, which are later accepted; the fighting comes to an end.

1919   International Peace Conference in Versailles.

        Daily airmail service begins between New York City and Chicago.

1921   July 2. World War I is officially declared at an end by Congress, and, later, the United States signs and ratifies treaties.

1927   Charles A. Lindbergh flies from New York to Paris solo in his aircraft, *Spirit of St. Louis.*

1929   October. Stock market crashes.

1930   The economy sags drastically, unemployment approaches 4 million and the period known as the "Great Depression" begins.

1939   Germany invades Poland and World War II begins, although the United States has not yet entered the war.

1941   December 8. The U.S. declares war on Japan and enters World War II the day after the bombing of Pearl Harbor.

        Scientists begin work on the Manhattan Project, development of the atomic bomb.

1945   May 7. Adolf Hitler commits suicide and Germany surrenders.

        August 6. The United States drops an atomic bomb on Hiroshima, Japan. About 135,000 deaths and injuries result. The United States drops a second bomb on Nagasaki and Japan surrenders on August 14.

        U.S. troops enter Korea south of the 38th parallel, replacing the Japanese.

1950   The United States recognizes the new country of Vietnam and sends military advisors to teach the use of weapons.

        The Korean War begins.

1957   Soviets launch the first artificial satellite, called Sputnik.

1961   In an orbital space flight, Soviet cosmonaut Yuri Gagarin becomes the first human in space, followed by Alan Shepard, the first U.S. man in space.

        The United States begins direct military support to South Vietnam.

1962   John Glenn becomes the first American to make an orbital space flight.

1963	President John F. Kennedy is assassinated.
1965	The United States sends troops to Vietnam.
1966	The United States Department of Transportation is established at cabinet level.
	78 million passenger cars and 16 million trucks and buses are registered this year.
1968	The United States and Vietnam hold peace talks in Paris, and the United States ends bombing in North Vietnam.
1969	Neil Armstrong and Buzz Aldrin become the first men on the Moon.
1973	The United States and South Vietnam sign a cease-fire with North Vietnam; the Vietnam War ends.
1974	Richard Nixon, plagued by the Watergate scandal, resigns as president of the United States.
1976	Gasoline shortages during winter months reduce use of automobiles.
	World's longest nonstop commercial airline flight is made by Pan-American, 8,088 miles in 13 hours 31 minutes.
1977	The energy crisis continues in the United States.
1978	New Panama Canal treaties are ratified, giving control of the canal to Panama at the end of 1999 and the United States the right to defend the canal's neutrality.
1979	The United States suspends Iranian oil imports in response to holding of 50 American hostages in Iran; energy crunch continues.
1980	U.S. population reaches over 226,500,000.
1981	U.S. hostages in Iran are released.
	About 13,000 air traffic controllers go on strike.
1981–82	Recession in the United States.
1983	October. U.S. troops land in Grenada, intervening in a coup there.
	Thousands of independent truckers go on strike in protest against increased fuel taxes.
1986	The United States launches nighttime air attacks against Libya in a tense standoff.
1989	Earthquakes in San Francisco severely damages San Francisco-Oakland Bay Bridge and freeway in Oakland.
	East Germany tears down the Berlin Wall, ending the "Cold War" period of antagonism and noncooperation between the Soviet Bloc and the West (including the United States).
	December. U.S. troops invade Panama and force the surrender of Panamanian General Manuel Noriega to stand trial in the United States on drug-trafficking charges.
1990	Iraq attacks Kuwait, causing another hike in gasoline and oil consumer prices in the United States.

GLOSSARY

aqueduct A bridge, usually made of wood, stone or steel, for carrying a canal and its boats (or sometimes just water) over a river, creek or other obstruction.

bulldozer An earth-moving machine to move heavy loads of earth with a large blade that can be raised or lowered.

canal An artificial waterway—a channel cut through land to carry water—especially one used for transportation.

canal boat A vessel that can be steered on a canal for transporting cargo or people.

cholera An acute, severe infectious disease affecting the intestines. It can be transmitted through food or water.

cut A trench carved out below the level of the surrounding ground (for example, through a hill) for a canal, road, railroad line, and so on.

drainage Removal of water from an area by providing channels, tunnels, pipelines and the like, or by pumping.

dredging The process of digging out mud and silt from under water to maintain a passage. Usually done from a barge or other vessel mounted with excavating machinery.

embankment A ridge of earth or gravel heaped up to provide banks for a canal.

engineer A person who plans, designs, builds and/or manages canals, roads, bridges, buildings, airports and other large structures.

epidemic A rapidly spreading outbreak of disease.

feeder canal A channel cut from a waterway to convey water to a canal or reservoir.

grade Steepness of a slope.

inclined plane A sloping railroad track fitted with cradlelike cars built to carry boats over steep or rough terrain. Used in areas where canal locks are impractical.

irrigation A way of moving water into areas that would be otherwise dry, through the use of canals and dams.

lock A compartment in a canal separated from the main stream by watertight gates at each end. As water fills or drains, boats are raised or lowered from one level to another. In this way, the canal's water and the boats on it can actually travel uphill and smoothly navigate otherwise steep downhill slopes.

locking through The process of moving into a lock on a canal, up or down from one level to another, and out again into the canal's main stream.

locktender The person who operates the lock whenever a boat comes through.

locomotive A self-powered engine that pulls or pushes railroad cars.

packet boat A canal boat that carries passengers only.

silt Fine-grained material (finer than sand) deposited on a canal or river bottom.

sluice An artificial passageway for draining off water.

sluice gate A valve or gate for controlling water flow through a sluice.

stationary engine A large steam engine, usually mounted in a shed, that pulls the cable of an inclined plane railroad.

technology The use of science to solve practical problems.

towline or towrope The rope used to tie mules and other tow animals to boats for towing.

towpath Path along the bank of a canal where mules and other tow animals walk, towing the boat.

BIBLIOGRAPHY

Bowman, Hank Wieand. *Pioneer Railroads.* New York: Arco, 1954.

Bruchey, Stuart. *The Wealth of the Nation: An Economic History of the United States.* New York: Harper & Row, 1988.

Chamberlain, John. *The Enterprising Americans: A Business History of the United States.* New York: Harper & Row, 1963.

Chidsey, Donald Barr. *The Panama Canal: An Informal History.* New York: Crown, 1970.

Condit, Carl W. *American Building.* Chicago: University of Chicago Press, 1960.

———. *American Building Art.* New York: Oxford University Press, 1960.

———, and Frances. *The Ingenious Yankees.* New York: Thomas Y. Crowell, 1976.

Fatout, Paul. *Indiana Canals.* Purdue, Ind.: Purdue University Studies, 1972.

Groner, Alex. *American Business and Industry.* New York: American Heritage, 1972.

Hadfield, Charles. *World Canals: Inland Navigation Past and Present.* New York: Facts On File, 1986.

Holbrook, Stewart. *The Old Post Road: The Story of the Boston Post Road.* New York: McGraw-Hill, 1962.

———. *The Yankee Exodus.* New York: Macmillan, 1950.

Hubbard, Freeman. *Encyclopedia of North American Railroading.* New York: McGraw-Hill, 1981.

Jacobs, David, and Anthony E. Neville, *Bridges, Canals & Tunnels: The Engineering Conquest of America.* New York: American Heritage, 1968.

Langdon, William Chauncy. *Everyday Things in American Life, 1776–1876.* New York: Charles Scribner's Sons, 1941.

Lingeman, Richard. *Small Town America.* New York: G. P. Putnam's Sons, 1980.

McCullough, David. *The Path Between the Seas: The Creation of the Panama Canal, 1870–1914.* New York: Simon & Schuster, 1977.

Meditz, Sandra W., and Dennis M. Hanratty, eds. *Panama: A Country Study.* Washington, D.C.: U.S. Government, 1989.

Merk, Frederick. *History of the Westward Movement.* New York: Alfred A. Knopf, 1978.

Miller, Douglas T. *Then Was the Future: The North in the Age of Jackson, 1815–1860.* The living History Library, John Anthony Scott, general editor. New York: Alfred A. Knopf, 1973.

O'Neill, Richard W. *High Steel, Hard Rock and Deep Water: The Exciting World of Construction.* New York: Macmillan, 1965.

Payne, Robert. *The Canal Builders: The Story of Canal Engineers Through the Ages.* New York: Macmillan, 1959.

Plowden, David. *Bridges: The Spans of North America.* New York: W. W. Norton & Co., 1974.

Rose, Albert C. *Historic American Roads.* New York: Crown, 1976.

Schlesinger, Arthur M., Jr., ed. *The Almanac of American History*. New York: G. P. Putnam's Sons, 1983.

Shank, William H. *Three Hundred Years with the Pennsylvania Traveler*. York, Pa.: American Canal and Transportation Center, 1976.

Shank, William H., ed. *The Best from American Canals, Number III*. York, Pa.: American Canal and Transportation Center, 1986.

———, ed. *The Best from American Canals, Number IIII*. York, Pa.: American Canal and Transportation Center, 1986.

———, ed. *Towpaths to Tugboats: A History of American Canal Engineering*. York, Pa.: American Canal and Transportation Center, 1982.

Smelser, Marshall, and Joan R. Gundersen. *American History at a Glance*, 4th ed. New York: Harper & Row, 1978.

Smith, Page. *The Shaping of America: A People's History of the Young Republic*. New York: McGraw-Hill, 1980.

Urdang, Laurence, ed. *The Timetables of American History*. New York: Simon & Schuster, 1981.

INDEX

Numbers in *italics* refer to illustrations.

A

Abbott's Landing, *11*
Adams, John Quincy, 42
airmail service, 72
Akron (Ohio), 28, 30
Albany (New York), 19, 25
Aldrin, Buzz, 73
Alexandre La Valley (boat),
 54
Allegheny Canal, 25
Allegheny Mountains, 32
Allegheny Portage
 Railroad, 32
American Philosophical
 Society, 13
Ancon (ship), 54, 61
Appalachian Mountains,
 15, 30
aqueduct
 definition of, 75
 Erie Canal, 19
Arizona, 42
Armstrong, Neil, 73
Army Corps of Engineers,
 54, 59
Atlantic Intracoastal
 Waterway, 68
atomic bomb, 72
Austin, Addison, 70
automobile, 64

B

Balcony Falls, *7*
Baltimore (Maryland), 13
Baltimore and Ohio
 Railroad, 33, 40, 42
bank notes, 47–48

barges, 65, *68*
bark, *6*
Bay Springs, 67, 69
Berlin Wall, 73
Best Friend of Charleston
 (locomotive), 35
Bishop, Joseph Bucklin, 60
Booth, John Wilkes, 42
B&O Railroad—*See
 Baltimore and Ohio
 Railroad*
Boston (Massachusetts),
 10, 25
bowmen, 23
bridges—*See also names of
 specific bridges*
 Erie Canal, 19, *20*
 low, 20
 railroad, 42, 64
 truss design, 33
Bristol (Pennsylvania), 37
Broadhead, Charles, 17
Brooklyn Bridge, 38, 64
Brooklyn (New York), 25
bubonic plague, 55
Buchanan (Virginia), 40
Buffalo (New York), 22, 25
bulldozer, 75
Burlington (New Jersey),
 13
Burr, Aaron, 45–48
Burr, William H., 61
Byrd, William, 13

C

California, 33, 53
Camden and Amboy
 Railroad, 37

Canada, 15, 66
canal, 75
canal boat, 75
Canal du Midi—*See
 Languedoc Canal*
Canal Record (newspaper),
 59
Canal Zone, 54, 55
Cape Cod, 8, 9
Cape Cod Canal, 68
capstans, 10
captains, 23
Carondelet Canal, 8, 9
Carrollton Viaduct, 33
Carter, Jimmy, 63
Caspian Sea, 4
Chagres River, 54
Champlain (Northern)
 Canal,
 29
Ch'ang-an (China), 4
Charleston Harbor, 9
Charles V, King of Spain,
 53
Chesapeake and Delaware
 Canal, 24, 37–39, 68
Chesapeake and Ohio
 Canal, 24, 38–40, *39*, 42
Chesapeake Bay, 5, 7, 37
Chicago (Illinois), 25,
 48–51, *49*
Chicago and Galena
 Railroad, 25
Chillicothe (Ohio), 30
China
 first canals, 4
 first locks, 2, 4
 inclined plane, 10
cholera
 definition of, 75
 epidemic (1832), 28–29

Cincinnati (Ohio), 29
Civil War, U.S., 42
Clark, William, 13, 26
Clermont (steamboat), 26
Cleveland (Ohio), 29
Clinton, De Witt, 16–17,
 21, 25, 28
coal industry
 Delaware Division
 Canal, 37
 England, 4
 Lehigh Canal, 35, 38
Colden, Cadwallader D.,
 9, 16,
 21
Colombia, 55
Columbia (Pennsylvania),
 31
Columbia-Philadelphia
 Railroad,
 29
Compromise of 1850, 33
Concord (New
 Hampshire), 12
Concord River, 10
Conewago Canal, 8
Confederate States of
 America, 42
Connecticut River, 8, 9–10
Constitution, U.S., 42
construction of canals
 early canals, 12
 Erie Canal, 17–19, 23
 Panama Canal, 53,
 55–61
 Tennessee-Tombigbee
 Waterway, 67, 69
cooks, 23
Cooper River, 7, 8
crossings, Erie Canal, 19
Croton Aqueduct, 25

Culebra (Gaillard) Cut (Panama Canal), 54, *58*, 59–61, *60*
cut, 75
Cuyahoga Falls, 28

D

Dabon, Pierre, 5
Darius I, King, 4
Declaration of Independence, 13
Deep Creek, 7
Deep Cut (Chesapeake and Delaware Canal), 37–38
Deep Waterways Commission, 66
Delaware and Hudson Canal, 24, 35, 38
Delaware and Hudson Company, 35
Delaware and Raritan Canal, 24, 37, 38
Delaware Division Canal, 37, 38
Delaware Railroad, 35
Delaware River, 13, 35–37, 38
Depression of 1836-1837
Illinois, 50
Indiana, 47
Dickens, Charles, 20, 32
Diesel, Rudolf, 64
Dismal Swamp Canal, 6–7, 8
Divide Cut (Tennessee-Tombigbee Waterway), 67, 69, *69*
drainage, 75
dredging, 75
Dred Scott Decision, 42
drivers, 23
Duluth (Minnesota), 65–67
Duncan, Joseph, 49, 51
Duryea, Charles, 64
Duryea, Frank, 64

E

Eads Bridge (St. Louis), 64
earliest canals, 1–4
Easton (Pennsylvania), 35, 38
Eddie Waxler (towboat), 69
Eisenhower Lock (St. Lawrence Seaway), *66*, 66
electric automobile, 64
electric lights, 64
embankment, 75

energy crisis, 73
Enfield Falls, 10
engineer, 75
England, 4
epidemic, 75
Erie, Lake, 29
Erie Canal, 5, *17*, 35
bridges, *20*
chronology, 25
construction, 17–19
first suggestion of, 9
at Lockport, *24*
locks, 2, *21*
Owsego Canal, 29
plans for, 15–26
skepticism about, 13
success of, 21–23, 39–40
towpath, *18*
as "training ground" for engineers, 23–25
workers on, 23
Erie Railroad, 25
Euphrates River, 4
Europe, 4
Ewing, Thomas, 28

F

Fairport (New York), *20*
feeder channel, 75
Erie Canal, 19
financing, 35
of Dismal Swamp Canal, 7
of Erie Canal, 16–17
of Indiana canals, 47–48
of Middlesex Canal, 11–12
of Ohio canals, 27–28
Fink, Albert, 42
Fitch, John, 13
Ford, Henry, 64
Fourteen Points, 72
France
Languedoc Canal, *1*
Franklin, Benjamin, 13, 37
Frémont, John, 33
French and Indian War, 13
Fulton, Robert, 26

G

Gagarin, Yuri, 72
Gaillard, David, 54
Gaillard Cut—*See Culebra Cut*
gasoline automobile, 64
Gatun (Canal Zone), *62*
Gatun Dam, 54, 61
Gatun Lake, 61
Gausler, W. H., 36

Geddes, James, 17–18, 25, 27, 31
Genesee River, 19
Georgia, 13
Germantown (Pennsylvania), 13
Glenn, John, 72
Goethals, George Washington, 54, 57, 59–60
Goethe, Johann Wolfgang von, 53
Gold Rush, 33, 53
Gooding, Henry, 51
Gorgas, Maria, 57
Gorgas, William Crawford, 55, 56–57
grade, 75
Great Canal System (China), 4
Great Depression, 72
Great Dismal Swamp Land Company, 6–7
Great Falls of the Potomac, 6
Great Lakes region, 15
Greece, ancient, 4
Grenada, 73
Gulf Intracoastal Waterway, 68

H

Hadley Falls Canal—*See South Hadley Falls Canal*
Han dynasty, 4
Havre de Grace (Maryland), 39
Hay, John, 55
Henry I, King, 4
Hill, James J., 56
Hiroshima (Japan), 72
historical headlines
1607-1803, 13
1804-1825, 26
1826-1850, 33
1851-1869, 42
1870-1914, 64
1915-1990, 72–73
Hitler, Adolf, 72
Hodges, Harry Foote, 61
hoggees, 23
Holbrook, Stewart, 10
Hollidaysburg (Pennsylvania), 31
hopper barges, 65
Horn Pond (Massachusetts), *11, 12*, 12
horses, *22*
Houston, Samuel, 33
Howe, William, 33
Huckleberry Finn (Mark Twain), 58

Hudson Railroad, 35
Hudson River, 15–16
Humboldt, Alexander von, 54
Huron, Lake, 29

I

Illinois, 48–51
Illinois and Michigan Canal, *48*, 49–51, *50*
bank notes, *49*
Illinois Central Railroad, 51
Illinois River, 5, 8, 49
Illinois Waterway, 68
I&M Canal—*See Illinois and Michigan Canal*
inclined plane
as alternative to locks, 10
definition of, 75
Erie Canal, 16
Indiana, 45–48
Industrial Revolution, 4
Intracoastal Waterway, 7
Irish laborers
Erie Canal, 18
Illinois and Michigan Canal, 50
Indiana canals, 47
Ohio canals, 28
irrigation, 75

J

James River, 5–6, 7, 40
James River and Kanawha Canal, 7, 38–40, *40, 41*, 42
bridges, 20
night travel on, 41
James River Canal, 8, 38
James River Canal Company, 5–6
Jamestown (Virginia), 13
Jefferson, Thomas, 16
Jeffersonville (Indiana), 45
Jervis, John P., 24–25
Johnson, Andrew, 42
Johnstown (Pennsylvania), 32, 61
Joliet, Louis, 5, 8, 49
Juniata River, 31

K

Kanawha Canal—*See James River and Kanawha Canal*
Kanawha River, 5

Kansas, 42
Kennedy, John F., 73
Korean War, 72

L

Lachine Canal, 66
Languedoc Canal, *1*, 4
larvacide, *57*
Lehigh Canal, 24, 35–37, *36*, 38
Leonardo da Vinci, *3*
Lépinay, Adolphe Godin de (Baron de Brusly), 59
Lesseps, Ferdinand de, 53, 54, 55
Lewis, Fielding, 8
Lewis, Meriwether, 13, 26
lift bridges, Erie Canal, *20*
limestone, 19, 24
Lincoln, Abraham, 42
Lindbergh, Charles A., 72
Little Falls Canal, 8
Little Falls of the Potomac, 6
locking through, 75
Lockport (New York), *21*, 22, *24*
locks
    Da Vinci's, *3*
    earliest, 4
    Erie Canal, 19, *21*
    inclined plane as alternative to, 10
    "lock" defined, 75
    Middlesex Canal, *12*
    operation of, 2
    St. Lawrence Seaway, 2
locktender, 75
    Erie Canal, 23
locomotive, 75
Louisiana Puchase (1803), 8, 13
Louisville (Kentucky), 42
Lowell (Massachusetts), 8, 10, 12
lumber, *11*
Lynchburg (Virginia), 6, 40, 43

M

Main Line Canal—*See Pennsylvania Canal*
malaria
    Erie Canal, 19, 25
    Panama, 55–56
Manhattan Project, 72
Marryat, Frederick, 23
Marshall, John, 8
Massachusetts, *6*

Mauch Chunk (Pennsylvania), 35, 38
Maumee River, 29, 46
McAlpine, William, 25
McCormick, Cyrus, 33
McCullough, David, 61
McKinley, William, 64
mechanical reaper, 33
Mennonites, 13
Merrimack River, 8, 10, 12
Mesopotamia, 4
Mexican War, 33
Miami and Erie Canal, *27*, 28–29, *29*, 46
Michigan, Lake, 5, 8
Middle East, 4
Middlesex Canal, *6*, 8, 10–12, *11*, *12*, *20*
Miraflores Lake, 59, 61
Miraflores Locks (Panama Canal), *63*
Mississippi River, 49
Missouri Compromise (1820), 26, 42
Mohawk and Hudson Railroad, 25, 43
Mohawk River, 15–16, 19
Montezuma Marshes, 19
Montreal (Quebec), 25
Morris, Gouverneur, 16, 25
Morris Canal, 10, 37, *37*, 38
Morrison, William, 64
mosquitoes
    Erie Canal, 19
    Ohio canals, 28
    Panama, 56–57
Muscle Shoals (Alabama), 24
Muscle Shoals Canal, 59

N

Nagasaki (Japan), 72
National Turnpike, 26
Netherlands, 2, 4
Newark (New Jersey), *37*
Newark (Ohio), 30
New Hampshire, 12
New Haven and Farmington Canal, 24
New Hope (Pennsylvania), 37
New Mexico, 42, 64
New Orleans (Louisiana), 9
New York City, 13, 15, 22, 25
New York State
    map, *16*
    tourism, 65
New York State Barge Canal, 68
Niagara Falls, 24

Nile River, 4
Nippur (ancient city), 4
Nixon, Richard, 73
Noriega, Manuel, 73
North Carolina, 6
Northern Canal—*See Champlain Canal*
Northern Indiana Railroad, 51
North Slope (Alaska), 62
Nuñez de Balboa, Vasco, 54

O

Ohio, 27–30, *30*, 35
    map, *27*
Ohio and Erie Canal, *27*, 28–30, 29
Ohio River, 5, 42, 45–46, *46*, 48, 64
Oklahoma Territory, 64
OPEC oil embargo, 62
Orléans Canal, 4
Oswego Canal, 2, 29
overland mail delivery, 33

P

Packard (automobile), 64
packet boat, 75
Panama Canal, 65
    chronology, 54
    engineering feats, 59–61
    first efforts, 53, 55
    Goethals role, 59–60
    present day, 62–63
    Stevens role, 56–59
    Wallace role, 55–56
Panama Canal treaties, 73
Panama invasion (1989), 73
Panamanian Revolt (1903), 55
Panama Railroad, 57
Pasquotank River, 7
passenger travel
    James River and Kanawha Canal, 41
    Middlesex Canal, *20*
Path Between the Seas, The (David McCullough), 61
Patowmack Canal, 8, 38, 39–40
Patowmack Company, 6
Pearson, Lester, 66
Penn, William, 13
Pennsylvania, 30–33
    map, *31*
Pennsylvania Canal, 10, 20, 24, 29, 31, 43

Pennsylvania Railroad, 43
Persia, 4
Philadelphia (Pennsylvania), 13, 25, 31, 64
Phillipsburg (Pennsylvania), 38
Pilgrims, 13
plague—*See bubonic plague*
Plymouth (Massachusetts), 13
Pontchartrain, Lake, 9
Potomac River, 6, 8
Potowatomis (Indian tribe), 46
Poughkeepsie Bridge, 64
Promontory Point (Utah), 42
Proprietors of Locks and Canals
    seal, *9*

Q

Quakers, 13
Quebecois (tanker), *67*

R

railroads, 35, 42–43—*See also names of specific railroads*
    Indiana, 46
    Isthmus of Panama, 53
Randle Jr., John,, 37
Reading Railroad, 39
Red Sea, 4
Rensselaer Polytechnic Institute, 26
Republican Party, 42
Revolutionary War, 13
Richmond (Virginia), 5–6, 13, 40, 43
Richmond and Allegheny Railroad, 42
Riverside Drive (New York City), 25
roads, 5
Roberts, Nathan
    Chesapeake and Ohio Canal, 40
    Erie Canal, 19, 22
    later projects of, 24
    Pennsylvania Canal, 31
Rochester (New York), 19, 22
Roebling, John A., 35, 38
Rome, ancient, 4
Roosevelt, Franklin D., 66
Roosevelt, Theodore, 54, 55–56, 58–59, 61
Russia, 4

S

Sacramento Deep-Water
    Ship Canal, 68
St. Lawrence Seaway, 24,
    65–67, *66, 67,* 68
St. Mary's City
    (Maryland), 13
St. Mary's Falls
    Canals—*See Soo
    Canals*
St. Petersburg (Russia), 4
San Francisco
    (California), 25
San Francisco-Oakland
    Bay Bridge, 73
Santee-Cooper Canal, 7–9
Santee River, 7, 8, 9
Schmidt, Donald G., 62
Schuylkill and
    Susquehanna Canal, 8
Schuylkill Navigation
    Canal, 29
Schuylkill River, 8
scrip, 47–48
Seneca Chief (boat), 21, 25
Senf, John Christian, 8–9
Shepard, Alan, 72
shingles, 7
silt, 75
Sixteenth Amendment, 64
slave labor
    James River and
        Kanawha Canal, 40
    Potomac canals, 6–7
sluice, 76
sluice gate, 76
Snell locks (St. Lawrence
    Seaway), 66
Soo (St. Mary's Falls)
    Canals, 29, 66
South Carolina, 7, 9, 35, 42
Southern United States
    early canals, 6–9
South Hadley Falls Canal,
    8, 9–10

Spanish-American War
    (1898), 64
Spirit of St. Louis (aircraft),
    72
Sputnik, 72
Standish, Miles, 8, 9
Stanley Steamer, 64
stationary engine, 76
steamboat, first, 13
steersmen, 23
Stephens, John Lloyd, 54
Stevens, John F., 54, 56–59
Suez Canal, 53, 55
    ancient forerunner of,
        4
Superior, Lake, 29, 66
Supreme Court, U.S., 42
Susquehanna and
    Schuylkill Canal, 24
Susquehanna and
    Tidewater Canal, 39
Susquehanna Canal, *32*
Susquehanna River, 8, 31
Sutter, John, 33
Syracuse (New York), 22

T

tank barges, 65
taverns, *11*
technology, 76
Tennessee-Tombigbee
    Waterway, *67,* 67–70, *68,
    69, 70*
Terre Haute (Indiana), 48
Texas, 33
Thirteenth Amendment,
    42
Thoreau, Henry David, 11
Toledo (Ohio), 29
tolls
    Erie Canal, 16, 21
    Middlesex Canal, 11
    Panama Canal, 62
Toronto (Ontario), 25

Torrijos, Omar, 63
tourism, 65
towline (towrope), 76
towpath, *18, 22*
    definition of, 76
towpath walker, 23
transcontinental railroad,
    42
Transportation, U.S.
    Department of, 73
Treaty of Paris (1898), 64
Trent River, 4
truss bridges, 42
    Ohio River, 64
Twain, Mark, 58
Tyngsborough (New
    Hampshire), 12

U

Union Canal, 8, 29
Utica (New York), 22

V

Venice (Italy), 4
Versailles Peace
    Conference (1919), 72
Vietnam, 72–73
Virginia, 5–6

W

Wabash and Erie Canal,
    46, 47–
    48
Wabash Railroad, 45–48
Wallace, John Findley, 54,
    55–56
War of 1812, 26
Washington, George, 8

Chesapeake and Ohio
    Canal, 38, 39–40
Indiana canals, 46
James River Canal
    Company, 5–7
Kanawha Canal, *7*
*Week on the Concord and
    Merrimack Rivers, A*
    (Henry David Thoreau),
    11
Welland Canal, 24, 66, 68
Westford (New
    Hampshire), 12
Weston, William, 10
West Virginia, 42
White, Canvass, 19, 24, 25,
    31–32, 36
White, Josiah, 35–36, 38
Whitewater Canal, 46, 47
Whitewater River, 46–47
Whitney, Eli, 13
Williamsburg Bridge (New
    York City), 64
Wilson, Woodrow, 72
Windsor Locks Canal, 10
Witham River, 4
Woburn (Massachusetts),
    11
World War I, 61–62, 64, 72
World War II, 72
Wright, Benjamin, 17–18,
    24, 25,
    37, 40
Wright brothers, 64
Wrightsville
    (Pennsylvania),
    39
Wyoming territory, 42

Y

yellow fever, 55–56
Yellow River, 4
York Haven Falls, 8